PRAISE F(

Warrior's ¦
THE JOURNEY HOME

BOB ANDERSON GREW UP seeking a personal discipline in his life. With his decision to join the Marine Corps, he found the discipline—and a brotherhood that would never leave him—in the combat environment of Southeast Asia. Applying this acquired discipline to the remainder of his life, he began seeking truths in religion and philosophies. He found common positive truths in every religion that he studied. Whether in his career in information technology, music, or life studies, he put everything into the effort. Fortunately, along the way, he met a soul mate in his wife, Vidya, who was equally dedicated. His book is the autobiography of a dedicated and disciplined individual whom I have been privileged to know for many years. — *Alan H Barbour, Historian, U.S. Marine Corps Combat Helicopter Association*

THIS IS THE SURPRISING and original autobiography of a warrior and spiritual seeker. From his service as a Marine in the Vietnam War to a successful career as a family man and business person, Robert Anderson's life is a search for spiritual truth. This search leads him to his Guru, and to a remarkable relationship between a soldier and an Indian spiritual master. The story of the two men is like that portrayed in the Indian spiritual classic, the Bhagavad Gita, in which a great warrior has God as his spiritual friend and advisor. Like the warrior in the Bhagavad Gita, Robert Anderson's devotion to his Guru is that of a friend and deeply devoted disciple. Robert Anderson's wisdom and devotion to his ideals is fresh and inspiring. — *Jeffrey Carr, Academic Dean of the School of the Pennsylvania Academy*

ROBERT ANDERSON'S SEARCH for Truth has its roots in his days of military training and service as a U.S. Marine. He emerged from the challenging combat conditions he faced in Vietnam armed with the necessary grit and strength to overcome the challenges in his life. Robert also realized he had a new yearning for Truth. Whether by fate, circumstance, or both, he met spiritual master Gururaj Ananda Yogi, a singular moment for Robert. In his description of becoming grounded in the wisdom and love of the Guru's

i

teachings, Robert will draw you into the realization of Truth. Written with a relaxed and conversational style, Robert's book will give you hope and, maybe, even bring you home. — *Joe Charsagua, Colonel, U.S. Army Reserve (Retired) and Certified Yoga and Meditation Instructor*

WARRIOR'S SONG: THE JOURNEY HOME is not the usual run-of-the-mill book you read for a pastime! It is an intense book about a brave man who stands for the values instilled in him by the U.S. Marine Corps—honor, courage, and commitment. The book describes the gripping journey of a real soldier written from the depths of his heart. Some books you put down and don't pick up again. Not this one. You may lay it down often while reading to contemplate a deep passage, but you will pick it up over and over until you are finished reading the last word! You will read it again and again, and every time you will get some new insight into your own life.
— *Murali Chemuturi, Author and Software Development Consultant, Chityala, India*

FROM HUMBLE BEGINNINGS as a boy, to a Marine warrior in Vietnam, to a top executive in a high tech industry, to a student and teacher of the ultimate truth of human existence, Bob "Suj" Anderson has travelled the world and done it all. More than an autobiography, *Warrior's Song* is a shining example of the triumph of the human spirit. In short, it's a delicious read, a movable feast. — *Dr. Stephen E. Langer, Physician and Author of* **Solved: The Riddle of Illness**

WARRIOR'S SONG: THE JOURNEY HOME is a rip-roaring read. Bob Anderson's incredible life story, as a decorated Vietnam Marine veteran, world-class businessman, and #1 disciple and devotee of one of the 20th century's greatest spiritual teachers, Gururaj Ananda Yogi, is an inspiring, page-turning tale of courage, adventure, spiritual faith, and successful living. Read this book—you won't be able to put it down! — *Lee Swanson, President, Swanson Health Products*

Warrior's Song

THE JOURNEY HOME

By Robert Anderson

Spirit Eagle Press ©2013

Spirit Eagle Press, Boiling Springs, PA 17007
© 2013 by Robert Anderson and Spirit Eagle Press
All rights reserved. Published 2013.

Printed in the United States of America

ISBN: 978-0-9895264-0-1

Credits and Permissions:

Book editor: Linda Weaver
Copy editor: Sharon Littlepage
Cover designer: Aaron Shugart-Brown

Robert Anderson has obtained permission to use the official symbols and insignia of the Marine Corps.

Neither the Department of the Navy nor any other component of the Department of Defense has approved, endorsed, or authorized this book.

Quotations at the beginning of chapters fall under the Doctrine of Fair Use of the U.S. Copyright Law.

PHOTOGRAPHS: Most of the photographs in *Warrior's Song: The Journey Home* were taken by Robert Anderson. Photographs taken by his family and friends are used with permission. Photographs of Gururaj Ananda Yogi are used with permission of members of the American Meditation Society. Photographs in Chapter 12 were taken by the Hubble Space Telescope and the public may use them.

CONTENTS

ACKNOWLEDGEMENTS

The United States Marine Corps
The character of the person within the pages of this book
was forged in the fire of discipline, honor, courage, and commitment,
which are the heart and soul of the Corps.

Gururaj Ananda Yogi
The spirit of the person within the pages of this book
was enriched and polished by my guide and best friend,
Gururaj Ananda Yogi. He showed me the glory of the Divine within
and guided my footsteps on the journey home.

Vidya Anderson
My loving wife, who worked tirelessly shaping the book
into what you read today.

Linda Weaver
My editor, without whose efforts this book would never be.

Brother Lee Swanson
… Because I love him.

Murali Chemuturi
My friend, who did a great job helping me over the rough spots
in refining the manuscript.

DEDICATION

To All Warriors on the Journey Home

PREFACE

The Warrior Within

War is not the primary theme of this book, but it was the catalyst for everything that came after in my life. The war chapters were not included to evoke excitement about warfare and killing. Rather, my telling a few "war stories" lets you know that I really do know what I am talking about—they put war in the context of something very significant in my young life.

War permanently shifted me toward reaching for a higher understanding of myself and life. The values I learned as a Marine directed my search for the common spiritual thread that we all share.

The warrior ethos has formed the core of my life and character during the forty-five-plus years that followed my service in Vietnam. Being a warrior does not mean only that you go to war and kill—it also has the much deeper connotations of Honor, Courage, and Commitment. These qualities define the warrior, whose calling is much more than "combat." It's a way of interacting with the world.

A warrior is one who overcomes obstacles or adversity to achieve an objective, a mission. It does not matter what the mission might be.

Being a true warrior is the willingness to do what you know is right and standing true regardless of the views of others. A warrior is committed to something or someone beyond self, to a greater good than one's own comforts or discomforts.

By this definition, the founding fathers of the United States of America were true warriors in the most perfect sense. They dedicated their lives—their positions, money, and sacred honor—to forging a nation that would stand the test of time and be a beacon of freedom to the world. I do not attempt to put myself in their league, but to the best of my ability, I have tried to live up to the principles of a true warrior.

The search for answers to the fundamental questions—*Who am I? Why am I here? Where am I going?*—I call the journey home. It has taken me through the horrors of war and around the world through many cultures and religions. We are all warriors traveling home, growing beyond the confines of our limiting concepts. Read the words within the pages of this book with an open mind and heart, but test everything in the crucible of your own life and experience. What works for you, keep. What does not work for you, discard. It is my sincere hope that *Warrior's Song: The Journey Home* will shine some light on your journey.

Robert Anderson
February 2013

CHAPTER ONE

A Marine in Vietnam

We have only to follow the thread of the hero path. Where we had thought to find an abomination, we shall find a god; where we had thought to slay another, we shall slay ourselves; where we had thought to travel outwards, we shall come to the center of our own existence; where we had thought to be alone, we shall be with all the world. — Joseph Campbell, American author and teacher of comparative mythology, in his book *The Hero with a Thousand Faces* (1968)

W e are all spiritual warriors singing creation's song, whether on the battlefields of Vietnam or in the daily routine of our jobs, or in our relationships with families and friends. The tension between creation and destruction describes so many of life's settings. It's surprising that the chaos and discipline of war set my life in motion and resonate so strongly more than forty-five years later. I still tune my life to them. Once a Marine, always a Marine.

War uncovered my spiritual voice, though I didn't realize it at the time, so it is fitting that *Warrior's Song: The Journey Home* open in the Southeast Asian Battlefields of Vietnam.

I graduated from Las Vegas High School in Nevada, where I lived in a small house in the desert with my mother, Irene, sister, Jody, and my Auntie Ann. Just prior to graduation, I decided to join the Marines. The call to adventure had hooked me.

 Part of wanting to become a Marine was that I didn't feel like I was ready for college yet. I'd had enough of books for a while. I was like any seventeen-year-old kid, adrift in the world wondering what I was going to do with my life. It was almost like an echo from the past that's hard to describe that drew me to the Marines. The toughest, the baddest, the best of the best, the first to fight, the last to leave, and leave no man behind.

All this resonated deep within my soul. Honor, Courage, and Commitment are the core values of the Marine Corps and are more than words to me. They set a standard of living that put others and the mission above myself and my personal safety. I loved those ethics and others such as innovate, adapt, overcome. Marines live and die by these watchwords.

We Marines believe there is nothing that cannot be overcome if you stick with it and stay focused, or die trying. It's a no-holds-barred, live-or-die approach to accomplishing the mission. In civilian life, job, family life, whatever…those character traits are engraved on our very souls, and become part of our personalities.

I didn't know all that when I first started. To me, it was just something new and exciting. On July 7, 1964, I got on a bus in Las Vegas and travelled to San Diego, California, to go to basic training (boot camp). Of course, the Marines never do anything by accident. We started off on the bus in mid-afternoon, so that by the time we reached the Marine Corps Recruit Depot (MCRD) in San Diego, it was 10 o'clock at night. The door opened and my world as I knew it came to an abrupt end. A drill instructor, uniform starched and pressed and wearing a Smokey the Bear hat, came storming up the stairs yelling and screaming, "Get out. Get out. Get out." The bus had picked up a number of recruits along the way. There were fifty of us by the time we hit MCRD.

Pronto we were standing on those little yellow footprints that all Marines know so well. Any Marine who reads this will understand the footprints. You see, we're too dumb to stand in a straight line, so they have us stand on yellow footprints in a line. They begin to berate and intimidate you in this way, and the process of tearing down your civilian personality begins. They keep you up all night long the first night, to begin the breaking down process. There is so much "in-processing" to go through that it takes several days.

They issue you yellow sweatshirts, tennis shoes, and green utility trousers, so it's easy to spot a new recruit. No combat boots yet. After in-processing, you are assigned to your platoon and series.

The Grinders

Suffice it to say that Marine Corps boot camp back in the 60s was very different from what it is today. Old timers will say, "That's not like the old Corps. You guys have it easy. You have nice barracks. We had Quonset huts that looked like half barrels, with concrete floors and steel racks with thin, 3-inch thick mattresses."

When they say you have to bounce a quarter off your rack—called a rack not a bed—that's the absolute truth! You learn to make hospital corners with six-inch folds on the top sheet. Got to be exactly six inches. Everything was discipline, precision, discipline, precision.

When we were issued our working clothes, or BDUs (battle dress uniforms but called "utilities" in my day), we had to stamp our names on everything with a black rubber stamp in a certain place, and stamp on the top inside lip of our boots in a certain place. On and on, and on and on...everything exacting to regulations.

Our bible was the *Guidebook for Marines*. It contained everything a new Marine needs to know about: what he does with his uniforms, certain aspects of Marine Corps history, close order drill, and a lot more. In the Marine Corps, you hear, "Do it by the numbers." That means when you are learning close order drill, you are so dumb and don't know what to do, that each movement is broken into steps. On the count of one you pivot, on the count of two you bring your heels together with your feet at a 45-degree angle. Whether it's the manual of arms or close order drill, it's repetition, repetition, repetition.

We used to march for hours on what we affectionately called the Little Grinder. There was also the Big Grinder, the large regimental area where we practiced for parades. On the Little Grinder we learned initial drill maneuvers. Once we learned the basic drills and weren't tripping all over ourselves—God forbid that should happen—we could go on to the Big Grinder where we could be seen by other platoons, other drill instructors, and officers. You didn't want to look like an idiot there; not only that, your drill instructor would skin you alive if you didn't look sharp.

Back in the day (my day), physical adjustment, let's call it, was a matter of course. For example, in those days we had the M-1 rifle for drilling. Then we changed over to the M-14 when we got to Camp Matthews, which was our rifle range for marksmanship qualifying. If you were doing a position within the manual of arms, and, for example, it is "Port Arms," you'd better have that rifle bisecting the angle between the head and shoulders at exactly 45 degrees, or the drill instructor would take your head and the end of your rifle and bring them together sharply. Hence, the term M-1 eyebrow, because you'd

4

get a scar just above your eyebrow where the site blade would cut in. But it wasn't brutality for the sake of sadistic brutality. You had to learn to be able to stand up under incredibly harsh mental and physical conditioning and even, to a degree, abuse. Let's face it. War is not a nice place. Our drill instructor told us once, on one of those occasions when he wasn't yelling and screaming at us, that the only thing worse than Marine Corps boot camp would be POW camp. How true!

The interesting thing was that though all of us hated it, our slack-ass civilian personas were completely torn apart, and we were built up as United States Marines. We were fit to be called Marines. We earned the right to wear the eagle, globe, and anchor—the official emblem of the United States Marine Corps—and to be part of a brotherhood of warriors that goes back to November 10, 1775, at Tun Tavern in Philadelphia, when the Marine Corps was founded.

It is the closest-knit brotherhood of warriors in the United States arsenal of freedom. It's mission first, your buddy second, and you a distant third; it's God, Country, and Corps.

That's the ethos of the Marines.

We'll scrabble amongst ourselves and we'll harass each other, but when it comes to any conflict outside the brotherhood, let no one mess with your brother and sister Marines. You might mess with them a little bit, but nobody else! Then you'll have to mess with every Marine in the neighborhood. The Corps is a family that in many cases is closer than blood family.

Regimental Honor Platoon

When we were in boot camp, our drill instructors were merciless. We had a Sergeant Sanchez and a Corporal Coggins. Sergeant Sanchez was the meanest thing on two feet, and also one the finest Marines and drill instructors that ever walked the Earth. Corporal

5

Coggins also was a superior drill instructor, like Sgt. Sanchez, and had the winning personality of a pit bull with a toothache. Coggins took all his direction from Sanchez who was the Senior DI. When you take a look at my boot camp photo, you'll see there's a platoon guide-on (flag) that says 361. From that little flag you'll see a whole number of little streamers, little silk pennants. Those are for competitions that Platoon 361 won.

'LADY LUCK' GROUP *Send back*

Vegas Marine Platoon Sets Recruit Drill Mark

Staff Sergeant Chuck Swindell of the local Marine Corps Recruiting Office has been informed that the Clark County "Lady Luck" Platoon, a unit which began active duty on July 7, recently set a new Marine Corps Recruit Depot record in drill evaluation.

The unit, along with all other recruit platoons undergoing training in San Diego, is evaluated each week to record their progress in all military subjects.

In the phase of Drill for Foot Troops, a segment of training essential for the furtherance of discipline and obedience to voice commands, the Clark County unit broke a Depot Record which has stood for two years.

IT WAS ALSO announced that the platoon topped all other units in their Series, a unit composed of four platoons, in the Third Week Military Inspection.

The "Lady Luck" Platoon is currently undergoing weapons and marksmanship training at the new Recruit Weapons Training Facility at Camp Stuart Mesa on Camp Pendleton, Calif., 38 miles north of San Diego.

DURING THE three weeks of training there, the new Marines will become acquainted with all of the small arms used by the Marine Corps today. They will also fire the standard Armed Forces rifle, the NATO 7.2 mm M-14, for qualification. In order to obtain the Marksmanship Badge, the recruits must fire a minimum score of 190 out of a possible 250 points.

While the unit is at Camp Pendleton, visitors are permitted to meet the recruits at the Reception Center at Camp Stuart Mesa on Saturday afternoon and - or Sunday afternoon. Relatives interested in visiting Camp Pendleton should contact the Marine Corps Recruiting Office at 130 South Sixth Street or call 382 - 9982.

Each platoon in a series of four platoons (which is a company) competes; then that series competes with other series and up and up and up until you get to the regimental level. You're scored on different military subjects like rifle range, close order drill, inspection, obstacle course, and physical training—ten or eleven categories. Our platoon took every single one and broke the drill evaluation record that had stood for more than two years in San Diego.

I'd give a thousand dollars to have a video of our "Drill Eval." We were wired tight and born again hard. It was quite an amazing thing that you have fifty-two guys, four ranks (squads) of thirteen guys, moving as if they were one—instantaneous response to command, absolutely letter-perfect on very complex close order drill maneuvers.

6

Boot Camp graduation, Platoon 361, Charley Company
Third Recruit Training Battalion

That's teamwork. That's what the Marine Corps is all about. It's not about the individual but the team. It's about the mission and protecting your buddies and their protecting you under any circumstances—up to and including combat! All that is drilled into you and indelibly impressed on your soul. It's not just mental. It goes down to the core of your personality; you undergo a transformation that lasts forever.

Rumors of War

I finished boot camp and went to the air wing instead of the infantry. I wanted to work with airplanes (which I loved) and things that go BOOM! So, I signed up for aviation ordnance (MOS 6511), which is explosives, rockets, cannons, and other things you can hang off various aircraft. As a sidebar, when you are in ordnance, you are also the armorer in your unit, which means I fixed all the rifles, pistols, and other small arms. After six months of school, I was ranked second

7

out of twenty-eight in the class. My confidence grew. I figured if I had survived boot camp, then I could do anything.

I went to my first duty station, which happened to be El Toro Marine Air Base in Anaheim, California. It's no longer there now, but then it was a thriving, huge base for the 3rd Marine Air Wing.

Certainly there were rumors of war. Vietnam was just beginning to kick into gear. It was August 1965 when I got to El Toro. When I reported to base headquarters, they asked me, "Is there any particular unit you would like to be posted to?"

In the Marine Corps it is very odd for them to ask you anything like that. So I immediately said, "Which is the next unit going to be deployed to Vietnam?" They said, "This photo reconnaissance outfit VMCJ-3 is due to rotate over within the next couple of months."

I said, "Put me in that one."

I wanted to get into the war. I wanted to see if I had what it takes to be a combat Marine because that's what Marines do—they fight. Marines go to war. I got into my squadron and further learned my trade. I worked with 20mm cannons, and for photo recon we had flares that were explosives that we had to manage on the aircraft.

8

In mid-September 1965, we packed up our gear. Before we rotated over, we had to dye all of our white underwear—excuse me, all of our skivvy shirts and shorts—forest green. Naturally, if you're walking around in white in a jungle war zone, you're a huge target, so we knew we were going to war when we were told to dye everything green.

We flew out of San Francisco to Okinawa, Japan. We stayed at Camp Butler for three weeks as they were processing us and giving us God knows how many shots to protect us as much as possible from all the diseases you find in a tropical jungle.

The flight to Okinawa was on a C-141 Starlifter, a huge four-engine jet with a high horizontal tail. After our three weeks of medical and administrative prep, we finally boarded a C-130 Hercules, which is a four-engine turbo prop. All of us were packed in there with helmets, rifles, packs, and all the equipment a Marine needs when he's being deployed forward. Forward deployment basically is a Marine

euphemism for "you're going to war." The aircraft was air-conditioned, but I'll never forget when we landed in Da Nang, just before the monsoon season started. The tail ramp of the C-130 went down, and it was like getting hit in the face with a wet blowtorch— must have been 100 degrees and 98 percent humidity. Unbelievable! The first things we got when we arrived were quinine pills for malaria and salt tablets, which we had to take immediately. Salt tablets were issued to replace the salt lost through excessive perspiration. We had to be sure we had a supply of those, and water, at all times.

We got on a "Deuce and a Half" (a 2.5-ton open truck), and they carted us over to what would be our living area. There were no structures, only a cleared out jungle with tents that were just being assembled. We threw all of our major gear into the tents.

I'd been flying for God knows how many hours and, lo and behold, I drew perimeter guard duty my first night in. I'd been up for eighteen hours as it was. So my first night in Vietnam was spent walking through elephant grass; I swear, it was up to my chest. My command post (CP) was an old concrete French bunker surrounded by concertina wire, which was razor sharp and had the tendency to jump out and snag you even if you just got close.

There was only one way to get through the wire—naturally, in the middle of the night, I got lost in it. After getting hung up in the wire I had to quietly call to my buddy Hank in the bunker to help get me un-stuck and guide me through the wire. It was a very embarrassing situation. I asked Hank not to tell the rest of the guys about my night of dancing in the wire. I would never have heard the end of harassment.

Both the corporal of the guard and officer of the day came out to inspect the posts. In the Marine Corps, there's a very formal way of reporting your post. In my case it was, "Sir, Lance Corporal Anderson reporting post number four. All secure. Post and orders remain the same. Nothing unusual to report." Then they would ask you one of your general orders. And you'd better know them. They were like learning your Ten Commandments in the Marine Corps. Of course, I knew them.

When the corporal of the guard came to check the post, he said, "Oh, by the

way, S2 (squadron intelligence) reported that we're supposed to get attacked at about 3 a.m., so keep it tight and frosty."
In others words, stay on high alert and on guard.

I thought, "Oh, that's sweet. My first night." I mean, it was pitch black, and if someone had been standing next to me and slit my throat, I would have known it only after it had already happened.

For some reason, the Viet Cong (VC) decided not to attack that night. However, we were on high alert all night long. From then on, it was 24/7. You'd work on your aircraft and do your normal job during the day, then stand perimeter guard at night. It was twenty- or twenty-two-hour days in many cases for weeks. We were just dead on our feet. During this time, the attack warning was given about five times when I was walking post. I began to think I was a VC magnet. After we got settled in, we got into a more livable routine, working only eighteen hours a day.

After a few months, I wrote a letter to my sister and it was published in the *Chicago Sun-Times.* My letter became the first in a series of "Letters from Vietnam" (which later became nationally syndicated in every major newspaper in the United States). Here it is.

Chicago Sun-Times, Sun., Dec. 19, 1965
Letters from Vietnam... 'Mud, Sweat, Blood'

Dec. 25 will be the first wartime Christmas since 1952. Thirteen years after Korea, the holiday season finds a new generation of American servicemen in full-scale combat overseas.

What will these men be thinking this Christmas, and what will they be facing? To give its readers some idea, the Sun-Times *this week will publish letters that Vietnam servicemen have written to relatives and friends in the Chicago area.*

12

The following letter was written from Da Nang by Marine Lance Cpl. Robert C. Anderson, 19, to his sister Jo Anderson, 6161 N. Winthrop.

DEAR JO:

Well, how is my little sister doing? I bet you are doing a damn sight better than I am. I will now gripe to you for a while how miserable life is over here. To start, it rains here almost continually, and mud is a foot deep in most places. I am living in a tent with some other guys damn near in the middle of a swamp. I have to sleep with a club by me to beat off the mosquitoes that lift the netting and try to carry me away. Plus I have to try to keep from drowning in the mud. I am soaked all the time and have about an inch of water in my boots. Today I got four hours sleep in the afternoon (the first sleep in over 47 hours). I work on my planes during the day and have guard duty at night. God, am I beat.

The other night when I had guard, I was out at the perimeter of the base, right next to no-man's-land where all

the Gooks are. We were supposed to get attacked at 3 A.M. when I was on post. There I was, stomping through swamps by myself, scared to death and hoping nobody would come up and cut my throat, as I couldn't see a damn thing it was so dark. One of them could have been standing right beside me and I would never have seen him.

To clean up, we take a bath out of our helmets—or just stand out in the rain, to wash some of the filth and grime that accumulate in three or four days. We don't wash any more than that because the water is rationed.

The chow isn't bad, if you like eating the same kind of C-rations they had in 1945.

When we sleep (or try to), we sleep with our weapons beside us. Man, if someone came up to me in the middle of the night and shook me to get me up! One of two things would happen. I would either shoot him or die of heart failure.

But some of the Marines have it 10,000 times as bad as I do. You should see some of these guys coming off patrol. Dead tired. Covered with mud, sweat and maybe a little blood. They have barbed wire tied around their boots to keep them together, and their clothes are torn and ragged from stomping through the brush. And some of them don't come back at all.

I have seen guys come in shot up and half blown apart by land mines. I talked to one Marine last night who had the same post I had the night before. And 45 minutes later he was dead. Killed by a sniper in the jungle. As long as I live I will never get used to, or forget, the things I have seen.

We are all working seven days a week and 18 to 23 hours a day. All of us are really dead.

I am not writing this letter to worry you or scare you. I just want you to get a small picture of what I and all the other Marines like me are going through. And if you see anyone yelling for us to get out of here, just tell him we are fighting for what we believe in and backing our country with our lives and those are as high as the stakes can go.

Just ask him what he believes in and how much hardship and suffering he's willing to go through for his beliefs.

This is the first and last letter I will write to you like this. I don't like writing these things myself, and I would like to forget most of them. But none of us can.

If you like, you can let someone else read this letter, to let people know what we are all going through over here. It is 100 per cent fine by me, as some of these people need something like this to knock their sense back in order.

I know this letter is written poorly and spelled rotten, but I think it gets the point across. I have to go now, as I have to save my candle for future letters. Bye for now. God bless you. All my love,
Your brother, Bob

Moderately Uneventful First Tour

My first tour was moderately uneventful. I spent a month in the guard platoon where we got to play infantry, or grunts, when we would go out on patrol with the medical teams and doctors to guard them as they went into the villages. You always had to be careful. Guerilla

warfare is just a nasty business. You could have a little old lady, seventy years old, stab you in the back with a bamboo stake. Or a little kid, five years old, who didn't know any better, walk into a bunch of Marines and let the pin go on a hand grenade and blow up himself and everybody else up. This was not uncommon. War really sucks; there is no glory, just pain, suffering…and death…lots of death.

For the most part, meals were out of green cans that were processed before I was born—C-rations from 1944. You'd go to the chow line in the morning and have what passed for breakfast: reconstituted scrambled eggs that were greenish yellow and grayish green sausage. Everything had some form of green cast to it that was not very appetizing. I think I lived on peanut butter and jelly sandwiches and Kool-Aid for six months. These supplies were readily available at the Mess Hall. Gallon cans of peanut butter were always open. It looked like dry wall sealing putty—tasted a bit like that also!

One time I was on mess duty, where you are assigned to the kitchen to help the cooks prepare the food and clean up. I was in the GI shack, a euphemism for where the garbage is. We'd get the garbage cans and put them on Deuce and a Half trucks. I had a military driver's license and I'd drive out to the garbage area. Before I could get there, Vietnamese locals would swarm over the truck and start picking through what we threw away, which they could live on for weeks

On one occasion, a stray dog in the garbage dump nipped me. I went back and talked to the corpsmen. They dressed it up and said, "Where's the dog?"

"What do you mean where's the dog?

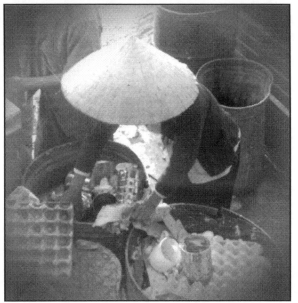

"I kicked his ass, and he ran the other direction." The corpsman got a smile on his face. Then he said, "Marine, you have just struck the jackpot. You have to go through rabies treatment."

"What's that?" I said.

"For two weeks you have to come here every day and we're going to take a needle, about three inches long, and inject duck embryo serum into the wall of your stomach."

They rotated the injections by quadrant because it was so painful. After about the third day, my stomach muscles were so sore I could not sit up. I had to roll over on my side and leverage myself up with my elbow. I was on a bit of light duty for a while. Not fun.

I was somewhat prone to unfortunate encounters with inanimate objects, too, as my luck would have it. Many Vietnam vets could tell the "No shit, there I was" war stories about getting wounded in combat. I have two.

I was disarming 20 MM cannons, working night flight operation when planes came back from night missions. I got back to my tent about 2 a.m. It was pitch dark, and I had to walk the length of the tent to get to my rack. I heard a fan running somewhere in the tent (we had just gotten electricity after four months).

I was trying to walk through the tent without hitting anything, then, whop! The fan clipped me on the side of my left knee. It didn't hurt that much, but I could see by dim moonlight that I had an extra mouth on the side of my knee with white bone showing through a bloody

gash. I shook one of the guys awake and asked him if he could help me to sick bay. About an hour later, the doc had sewed up my knee in layers. I still did my work, but with a serious limp and had to put up with a ration of razzing for being such a klutz.

The next not-so-combat wound was when I slit open my right index finger opening a can of tuna fish using a P38 (C-ration can opener). The photo of the

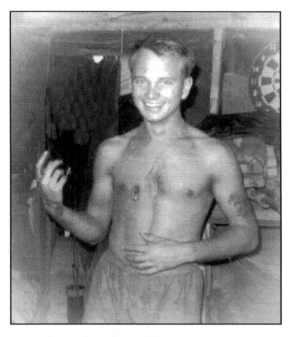

bleeding finger gash and the one of me showing off 20mm cannon ammunition captured my shit-eating ear-to-ear grin. Was it bemusement or hysteria? I don't remember exactly what I was feeling. The weirder things got, the more I seemed to smile. Life in the swamp was full of fun and games—and paradox.

A Door Gunner in Combat

Time passed. I'd had some interesting experiences, but I hadn't seen any real fighting. I was determined to get into combat.

As my first tour was coming to an end (thirteen months), I heard there was a helicopter outfit, Marine Air Group (MAG) 16, right on the beach at a place called Marble Mountain. A buddy of mine, who had

19

become a real good friend, and I said, "Let's go over and take a look at the place." We found an outfit called VMO-2, Marine Observation Squadron 2. At that time, they were the only outfit that had helicopter gunships in the Marine Corps. The helicopters were the Bell UH1-E Huey. They had rockets on either side, four external machine guns (two on each side), and two internal guns—one for the crew chief and one for the gunner.

I said, "Well now, goodness me, that looks really interesting, real kick-ass Marine stuff." I went into the squadron office and requested to see the first sergeant to ask him if I could get an appointment with the XO (the executive officer) who was responsible for all personnel.

"Sir, I'm in weapons and ordnance, and I really want to be a door gunner and get into combat. I've just completed one tour, and I've got excellent Pro and Con marks [proficiency and conduct]. I'm good at what I do. I work hard. I'll extend another tour if I can come here and, as part of my duties, become a door gunner on a helicopter."

He said, "We'll see what we can do."

Later on, I got word from the first sergeant of VMO-2 that they would have a billet (my job specialty) for me, but not for a couple of months after my original squadron rotated back.

While waiting for the billet to open up, I went to H&MS 11, Headquarters and Maintenance Squadron for MAG 11 (Marine Air Group 11)—humping bombs. While I was waiting for my position to open up in VMO-2, I hauled ammunition, bombs, and rockets from the magazine to various squadrons. I had to drive through a couple of small Vietnamese villages, where VC were known to hide within the village population. If a grenade had landed in the back of the truck, I would not have been even a greasy spot on the road. Fortunately, that did not happen. Otherwise, this book would now be channeled by some spiritual medium—I would have been a very pissed-off ghost.

Finally my spot in VMO-2 opened up, and I moved from MAG 11 to MAG 16 down by the beach. It took a while before I started flying, though. I was in charge of all the machine guns, building all the rockets that go in the tubes, and safing and unsafing the aircraft as they flew in and out. That meant that I stood at the end of the taxiway where the helicopters would come off the active runway and hover as they moved into the helicopter parking area. I would have to put metal blocks into the machine guns to make sure the bolt couldn't go home and fire a round inadvertently; and put safety grounding pins on the rocket pods so no stray voltage would inadvertently set off a rocket. While I was doing that, there was a 60-mile-an-hour downdraft from

21

the main rotor going full tilt as they were hovering—I was literally getting sandblasted, because my position was right on beach sand. I was wearing goggles and Mickey Mouse ears that were very poor sound protection, though better than nothing. You've got the whine of engines, the sound of the rotors, the downdraft, and sandblasting. Suffice it say, it was part of the job, and we all did our jobs regardless.

I got my flight physical, was issued flight gear, and I got some basic aerial gunnery training. We'd fly out over the South China Sea, which was right next to us. We'd learn how to lead targets, when to fire (depending on how the pilot was turning), and all about in-flight radio protocol. All this time the activity of war was going on all around us—and escalating. You'd go to sleep by the sound of artillery going off at night; you'd go to sleep by the light of flares dropping to light up the whole countryside.

I remember standing on the flight line one evening watching something called "Puff the Magic Dragon," which was an old C-47 called a Gooney Bird that had been converted into a gunship. They put these miniguns in them. A minigun fires a 7.62 MM cartridge like an M-14, but at a rate of fire of 6,000 rounds per minute. The pilot would take the Dragon into an orbit called a pylon turn, banking at an angle. Then, the crew would bring the minigun to bear on a certain area and just cut loose. Every fifth round was a tracer, but it looked like a solid red finger of light, a laser beam going from the plane to the ground. They could put a bullet every inch in an acre of land in about a minute. We used to call it "The Finger of God." Those were the things you would go to sleep by and wake up to every morning.

Dropping Recon Team Behind Enemy Lines

One night we were flying a couple of recon guys wearing hundred-pound packs, all in grease paint—real jungle fighter stuff. They were scout sniper recon. We were flying in behind enemy lines, which we weren't really supposed to be doing, but that was their job—reconnaissance. We were screaming back and forth to each other because of all the noise of the rotor and the engine.

I was behind my machine gun sitting by the open door as far outside as I could go. These two grunts (sniper and spotter) were sitting between the crew chief and me. We were yelling back and forth trying to hold a mini-conversation. This grunt was telling me, "I wouldn't do what you do for anything in the world. You're just sitting here like a target duck in an open doorway, flying low and slow."

I was kind of laughing at him and said, "Yeah, but if I make it back from this mission, I'm going to sleep in a dry rack tonight. You are going to be in the damned jungle behind enemy lines for five days." We each had a real appreciation for what the other guy was doing.

At that point, I considered myself a real combat Marine. I'd gotten what I asked for. I was in combat.

While flying combat missions I was seldom really afraid, even when the bird was taking hits. A little tightness in the gut, but for the most part it was just a rush of adrenalin. So much was always going on—between the pilots jinking around the sky, going into dives, pulling up; me covering the zone; rockets going off; the powder from the rocket motors hitting me in the face—there was just no time to be afraid! Sometimes we'd come back and, on the lower part of my face not covered by my visor, I'd have an outline of black soot from the rocket motors. As they would go out of a tube, I'd get some of that back blast. I would be leaning forward trying to swivel my gun as far forward as possible so I could shoot with the pilot to bring more firepower to bear.

That didn't happen often. You'd always check with the HAC (Helicopter Aircraft Commander) before you did anything. But if he said go ahead and fire, hell man, we would just unload. There were times when, damn, I was throwing grenades out, and I was throwing empty cans and boxes. Anything. If I ran out of ammo and I could hit some poor damned VC with an empty or full C-ration can and give him one hell of a headache, that was good enough.

That was our life. You were either working on the aircraft or you were flying combat missions. Within a month, I started flying out of other bases: Dong Ha, Phu Bai, and Khe Sanh (which we will talk more about later).

CHAPTER TWO

War Times Two

The most noble fate a man can endure is to place his own
mortal body between his loved home and the war's
desolation.— Lt. Col. Jean V. Dubois in *Starship Troopers* (1959),
a book of science fiction by Robert A. Heinlein (1907-1988)

The following accounts describe some of my most notable
combat experiences in Vietnam during the years 1965 to 1967.
Several dozen more come and go in memory, but these are the
ones that for some reason seem to stand out. They are still vivid and
clear today, as if they had happened only a moment ago. Some
experiences in life indelibly mark the body, mind, and soul.

March 1967—Night Flight Operations

My helicopter received a frag order (operational flight order) to
escort a CH-46 on a resupply mission to grunts under heavy attack
from an enemy of unknown size. It was a night mission, Terry
Bowman was crew chief and I was door gunner. When we got on
station and were orbiting around 1,500 feet, the CH-46 set down in the
LZ (landing zone), and I could see the mortar rounds hitting around the
CH-46 as they frantically unloaded ammo and took on wounded. I
could see all this very clearly as we were in a left orbit and I was
facing the ground as parachute flares lit up the night.

All of a sudden over the IC (intercom for the air crew) the grunts
yell at us that we are taking heavy ground fire. I look out the door and
could see the tracers coming up toward my head. The bird shuddered a

little; then I looked between the HAC (helicopter aircraft commander) and co-pilot and saw all the little yellow and red lights coming on the instrument panel. I later found out we took rounds in the transmission/ engine compartment. So here was the situation: Flying at night, 1,500 feet above enemy territory, black as pitch, nothing but jungle canopy

below, no place to land, losing rotor RPM, and all the bad lights coming on the instrument panel. At that particular moment, my heart nearly stopped.

At squadron reunions, Terry and I talk about that night. I am very glad we both made it out alive and unhurt. It is a testament to good luck and the excellent job Terry and others did maintaining the helicopter in top running order.

I can still see that instrument panel as clearly today as I did that night, usually in the middle of the night waking up in cold sweats. Naturally, we hobbled back to base. In the morning, we discovered there were a number of bullet holes in the engine cowling (a hydraulic leak, but not a complete break in the line or I would not be writing this). There was a hole completely through the skid and through the floor on my side (left-gunner station) about six inches from my gun mount, which was right next to where I was sitting.

April 1967—Khe Sanh

My aircraft was flying out of Khe Sanh. We were supposed to be there for only three or four days flying med evac escort and recon inserts and extractions around the Iron Triangle (Laos, Cambodia, and Vietnam). During this time, the base commander was talking to my pilot and mentioning that they had just lost their ordnance specialist for the base. My pilot kindly mentioned that my MOS (specialty) was

ordnance. The base commander requested that I be reassigned temporarily to the grunts atop that little hill to make sure the base had enough stuff to shoot and blow things up with. My pilot asked me if I would volunteer to go TAD (temporary additional duty) to the base to help out until they were able to get someone assigned to handle ordnance. Naturally, I said yes. As a Marine, it was unthinkable for me to say no. So then I was really doing Marine combat stuff. One of the first things I heard while getting settled into a tent was, "Sleep with your rifle locked and loaded, safety on." The reason was that VC sometimes crept through the wire and put a satchel charge (explosives) by a tent or bunker and blow it and the Marine inside into tiny pieces. The next thing I heard was, "Oh, by the way, the word from the recon patrols is that the base is surrounded by two divisions of NVA regulars (North Vietnamese Army)." Welcome to Khe Sanh! What in the world had I gotten myself into? I wanted combat and I had it—in spades!

Part of my duties while at Khe Sanh was getting all ammo, grenades, and other explosives from the runway and into the bunkers before the mortars dropped.

When a C130 re-supply aircraft would do a hot landing and dump pallets of munitions on the runway, then beat feet back into the air as fast as their little props would lift them, I would run out on the runway. It was my job to grab a case of explosives and run my butt off getting to the ammo bunker before the mortars and rockets started to strike. The NVA knew when a plane landed that, most likely, supplies and munitions were involved. So it was standard procedure to get mortared while trying to get the explosives off the runway and into the bunkers. Dodging mortars while carrying a load of high explosives was interesting, terrifying, and life-changing—all at the same time! It was a challenge to keep from getting blown into tiny little pieces while getting ammunition off the runway to safety ASAP. Adrenaline was running in overdrive!

I was assigned to Khe Sanh for a little over a month. We never had the luxury of a full night's sleep. For thirty days I kept a bayonet under my pillow when I attempted to sleep, and my M-14 locked and loaded (safety on) next to my rack (cot). My tent was next to a 105 MM Howitzer battery. Every time they got a fire mission in the middle of the night, when the first volley was fired, it would lift me at least six inches off my cot—without me moving a muscle! OK, that might be a bit of an exaggeration, but not by much.

When I left Khe Sanh, I had to throw my utility uniforms away because what was originally olive drab when I arrived became a dark ochre red because they were so saturated with the red clay from the mountaintop.

May 1967—Combat Flying, Infantry Close Air Support, Hanging Over the Edge!

We had been flying one mission after another for about four or five hours, most pretty uneventful. However, just as we thought we were going back to base after one mission, the pilot got a call requesting that we provide fire support to the grunts who were receiving heavy fire from a VC-controlled village. Obviously, we were on our way. We rolled in on a staffing run at about 1,500 feet, all guns blazing. The pilot was firing the four external guns. The crew chief and I had swiveled our mounted M60s as far forward as we could, sat on the edge of the bench seat, and cut loose. We had six machine guns blazing at the same time. We rolled out on the crew chief's side; he covered the zone, keeping the bad guys' heads down.

We were getting ready for our next run when I looked at the external M60s on my side and saw one of the guns was hung up with a shell casing only partially extracted from the breach. The gun would not fire. I told the pilot about the situation. Since my MOS was in ordnance and weapon repair, he asked if I could fix it in flight. I looked at the gun and thought if I could just get the operating handle moved to the rear, the spent casing just might eject. I requested the pilot exit the zone and fly straight and level, and I would try to clear the jam.

I had my gunner's belt (four-inch heavy leather belt hooked to the aft bulkhead of the aircraft and around the waist of the gunner) in place and crawled outside the helicopter, slid down to the skid, and wrapped one leg around the skid. One hand was on my M60 gun mount, my other hand on the barrel of one of the external M60s. We were flying about 2,000 feet above the jungle, in a combat zone over enemy territory, at about 90 to 100 knots. I was hanging completely outside the helicopter, a sitting duck for any observant VC to take pot shots at.

I kicked the operating handle lever with my right boot heel, missing on the first try and almost losing my grip!

My arms ached carrying my weight, but somehow I steadied myself, then kicked a second time and hit it. The operating handle came to the rear and ejected the spent casing.

All of a sudden I heard BANG, BANG, BANG coming from somewhere on my side of the helicopter. I thought, "Damn, we are taking hits and here I am hanging out in the breeze." I was frantically communicating over the IC with the pilot, and then I looked back and saw my gunner's belt flapping on the side of the helicopter.

I quickly told the pilot that we were not taking hits—what a momentary relief!

But then, I realized that I was not attached to the helicopter except for one leg wrapped around the skid and hands clutching my gun mount (I had let go of the barrel of the external gun). I had failed to push the locking pin through the latch in the gunner's belt.

When I crawled out onto the skid, I tripped the latch and the belt came off without me knowing this at the time. I have never been so terrified in my life; I slowly crawled back into the helicopter with rotor wash and wind trying to tear me away from my precarious hold on the aircraft. Finally I managed to get strapped back in and we flew back into the battle zone with all guns blazing (including the one I just fixed) and completed the mission.

The pilot was quite angry, because if I had fallen, he would have had a mountain of paperwork to fill out and submit.

I never forgot to push the locking pin through the latch after that.

May 1967—Dong Ha—Bombardment

We were flying operations out of the base at Dong Ha; it was a typical evening, hot and humid. We had just finished up flight operations for the day and had eaten chow. It was somewhere around 1900 when the mortars and rockets (81 MM mortars and 120 MM rockets) began to hit the base. It appeared that the NVA, or VC, was trying to destroy the flight line where the helicopters were parked. When the sirens went off, I was on the flight line working on a Huey

31

with an M60 that kept jamming. I looked up and all I could see were guys running in all directions trying to get into a sand bag bunker. Rounds were getting pretty close by the time I finally got to a bunker close to the flight line. The bunker was about three feet underground with about four feet of sand bags above ground. There were at least fifteen guys huddled into that very small cramped space looking terrified

I took one look inside the bunker and decided that if this was my time to go I was not going to go while in a stinking hole. So I took a pint of Suntory (Vietnamese version of Wild Turkey whiskey) from a friend, climbed up on top of the bunker, and watched the flight line as rockets and mortars hit about 100 to 200 yards from where I was sitting.

The interesting thing is that none of our Hueys were damaged, but there were a number of craters blown into the ground not far from our flight line.

I think this was when I just got tired of all the insanity of war and all the pain of lost friends. I just didn't give a damn if a rocket or mortar hit me directly on the head—I think some part of me was hoping that one would. Eventually the "all clear" sounded; then everyone came out to see how much damage was done. Could have been a lot worse! All the guys in the bunker looked at me a little strangely as I dug a piece of shrapnel out of a sand bag with my bayonet near where I was sitting. I had that piece of shrapnel in a small glass bottle for many years, but it got lost somewhere. Damn! Sometimes dying is easier than living. It may be difficult for someone who has not gone through the horror of war to understand that many of the deepest and most profound wounds are those that no one can see.

Ambushed on the Ride Back to Dong Ha from Khe Sanh

I was nearing the end of my second combat tour. On the way back from Khe Sanh to Dong Ha, I hitched a ride in a convoy heading to Dong Ha because there were no helicopters coming up for several days. Naturally, my luck was twisted, as usual. Going through the jungle, I was riding "shotgun" (right seat) in a fuel truck and we were attacked.

There I was in a truck full of highly flammable gasoline, with hot rounds flying all around us. The first thing I did was get my ass out of the truck and into a ditch. Because of what I'd learned, being in charge of ordnance at Khe Sanh, I had loaded up before I left. I looked like Pancho Villa on steroids. I had two bandoliers of 7.62 FMJ (full metal jacket) for my M-14, four fragmentation grenades, a white phosphorous grenade, yellow smoke, red smoke, and six magazines of twenty rounds each. I was a walking ammo dump! I wanted to make sure that if anything happened I wasn't going to run out of anything. A patrol moved into the tree line and took care of whoever was shooting at us, or simply scared them away. We finally got back on the road to Dong Ha without further incident.

33

Back to the USA and the Land of the BIG PX

As my second tour was winding down, the Corps let me go back to the USA a month or so early—which really was nice of them. I wound up with twenty-two and a half months in country, and by that time I'd had my fill of combat and was more than ready to go back to the "Land of the Big PX" (USA).

They shipped me to the Marine Corps Air Station (MCAS) at Yuma, Arizona, to finish out the rest of my tour.

Naturally they tried to get me to reenlist. You could see in my military records that I was silly enough to volunteer for just about anything including combat, silly enough to volunteer to be a door gunner, silly enough to volunteer for a second combat tour. So they figured, "This guy is a good Marine!" And I was. They offered me money and rank, but I said, "You know, I think I've learned what I needed to learn."

Although there were times when I thought very seriously about making a career out of the Marines Corps, I suppose it was fortunate that I didn't, because I surely would have been killed somewhere. I had a bad habit of volunteering for dangerously stupid things, running into harm's way where angels fear to tread. I thought I was invincible.

Crazy!

When I checked in at MCAS Yuma, given my combat record, I guess they thought they would cut me some slack (take it easy on me). A lot of guys came back from Nam wounded, or somewhat as mental basket cases. By that time, because I had seen enough combat, I was a little twitchy, too. They put me in special services, which basically meant they put me to work at the PX, or the USO Club.

They made me noncommissioned officer in charge of base swimming pools, i.e., a lifeguard, which was really good duty. My job was to look at pretty girls and make sure nobody drowned. That is how I spent my last year in the Corps. I did turn it to my advantage. I became a Water Safety Instructor (WSI) for the Red Cross, which is no small thing to achieve. It's a tough course. If anyone tells you that he or she is a WSI, know that person worked hard for it.

I was training lifeguards and teaching swimming. Then, at the end of June 1968, I was discharged from the Corps. My mother picked me

up in Yuma, and we drove 300 miles back to Las Vegas, a six-hour drive, and I was back home once again.

CHAPTER THREE

Enrico Caruso and the Boy Who Went to War

The only thing that interferes with my learning

is my education. — Attributed to Albert Einstein (1879-1955)

The fighter and the lover in me began struggling for balance early in my life, long before I ended up in a combat zone in Vietnam. I was born at 3:15 a.m. on November 1, 1946, in Chicago, where I lived for five years until my parents divorced. I don't remember much from those days, except sitting with my mother and sister and listening to *The Shadow* and *Kukla, Fran, and Ollie* on the radio.

My sister was Jolene Ann Anderson—she likes to be called Jody nowadays. I was Robert Charles Anderson Jr. Technically I was the third. My father and grandfather were Robert Charles Andersons, too.

I moved with my mother and my sister to Delray Beach, Florida, to live with my Auntie Ann, as we called her. I lived there until I was eleven years old. While there, I became an altar boy in the Catholic Church. I seemed to excel at learning languages, and I began learning Latin in church at age seven. I was also in the choir singing Gregorian chant. That was my first exposure to singing, which took on a life of its own later in life.

When I was in school, I was always a dreamer. I was the kid who sat at the window and looked up at the sky. This world was not as real as the world inside my mind where the clouds turned into dragons and unicorns. I was an introspective child. In first grade I was told to stop daydreaming.

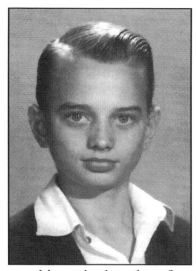

Later in life, I realized that my early schooling killed the dreamer in me and choked off the creativity that came naturally to me. That's truly sad, because in daydreaming I found a lot of internal joy—in that place free of the do's and don'ts, shoulds and oughts, and where I was free to roam and believe in things unseen but felt. I was instilled early in life with the idea that it's a dog-eat-dog world. I learned that I had to study and be smart or I wouldn't be able to earn a living and I'd end up living on the streets. I was instilled with a fear for survival. Whether

it's from our parents or from the social structure we live in, many of us get the message that life is all-competitive—a combat zone.

I understand that to some degree this kind of awareness is important, but unfortunately, along the way we kill the dreamer within us. I became very practical and lost most of my ability to daydream, to see images in the sky, to hear the song of the siren in the seas. I lost it, I lost it. What a shame.

As a child, I was a natural vegetarian, as I had no liking or desire to eat meat. I hated it. I preferred mashed potatoes, peas, vegetables, and fruit. I remember my mother serving me meat, and her typical "mother thing" that you can't leave the table until you clean your plate. I remember tucking a piece of roast beef into the corner of my mouth just so I could leave the table. I still had it in my mouth when I went to bed and when I woke up in the morning. My natural tendency was to eat things that were lighter and easier to digest. But then, conditioning comes in—you eat meat because that's what we do. It took me a long time, but as I ate more meat, I eventually began to like it.

We didn't have much money. My mother could innovate, adapt, and overcome in the best Marine tradition before I knew anything about those values. She would virtually do everything with nothing. And I learned how to do the same.

Even as a young child, the warrior in me was trying to get out. I would dress up as a Roman soldier—sword, shield, and all—for Halloween. Interesting, because my birthday is the day after Halloween on All Saints Day.

I was a solitary young boy. I would get cardboard boxes from furniture stores, and since I had engineering tendencies, I poked holes in the boxes with a screwdriver and sewed the boxes together with twine to make castles. I cut out windows and put strings on them so you could open and close them. I made tunnels and parapets. If you don't have a lot of money, you make do. You create things in your head and use the things at hand to entertain yourself. For example, at seven or eight, I swore I could fly. I had watched Superman on television and said to myself, "I can do that. It seems pretty easy to me." I got a small blanket and made a cape, then climbed onto the back porch roof and jumped off. I found out very quickly that gravity wins every time. Fortunately, nothing was broken. So much for that idea, but it was a worthy experiment.

At the age of around seven, while we were still living in Delray Beach, Florida, I had a vivid feeling that I came from somewhere else, and that the Earth was not my home. As weird as this may sound, it's something that has stayed with me a good part of my life and is probably lurking inside me even today.

One day I went into the back yard kicking the dirt around to find the latches to the doors of my imaginary buried spaceship. I actually thought that if I just found the right spot, the doors would magically open and I could go home. I have no idea what that means, and I'm sure some Freudian psychologist would have a ball with that one.

The idea of looking for home would manifest again and again in my later life but in quite different and unexpected ways.

My mother was a waitress. So was my Auntie Ann. When I was about nine years old, my aunt moved to Las Vegas and homesteaded five acres in the middle of the desert. The only way to get into town was on a dirt road that led to the main highway.

Auntie Ann had a windmill for water. No power. A septic tank. Gas lamps for lighting. And a generator she'd turn on every once in a while for power. She went to Las Vegas because everyone knew at the time that when you were in the waitressing business, Las Vegas was the place to be. The hotels had big restaurants with show rooms where tips were very good. Waiters and waitresses, now called servers, lived on tips and made a pretty good living back then.

Auntie Ann had been a sergeant in the Army during World War II, and she built her desert home by herself and turned it into a little oasis. She was amazing.

When I was eleven years old, Auntie Ann asked us to move out to Las Vegas to be with her, because she felt my mom could get a job and make better money in the resort industry. My mother, sister, an old family friend, our dog, and I drove from Florida across the country in a '55 Chevy station wagon. After a week of driving, we found ourselves in Vegas. It was June 1957—the desert was hotter than the door hinges of hell!

My mother got a great job as a waitress on the Las Vegas strip in the famous Sahara Hotel and Casino. Suddenly I went from running around in the surf on the coast of Florida to 110 degrees in the shade in the middle of a barren desert! I said, "Oh my, I've been dropped into hell. What did I do to deserve this? Holy crap! Sagebrush, Gila monsters, horned toads, sidewinder snakes, and not another human creature for miles!

There were also washed-out ravines from flash floods.

But there we were. This was the first huge, "Oh shit, I am screwed" in my short life—with many more to come.

Sometimes I would walk by myself into the desert, with a little bottle of water, and roam the dry riverbeds (washes) and desert flat lands. I felt like Moses. It was absolutely stone quiet. I was only a mile or so away from the house, so it was fairly easy to see where I was; I could always see the windmill, so I could get my bearings. The walls of the dry riverbeds, eight feet high, were made by torrents of flash-flood water. Once again I had my flash that I had to get home, "My spaceship is here! I just have to find it in the wall of this dry river bed." I kept looking for some twig, some branch, that would be a lever that would open the doors and there would be my spaceship and I could go home—a feeling of other worldliness would overcome me.

"Where is home? Where is home?" I would ask myself.

To my undeveloped mind, "home" took on the image of another planet (today many people who know me would probably agree with that), but as I grew older, I would find that home meant something much more profound and adventurous than any Buck Rogers story could ever be.

Perhaps I took to discipline in the Marines because Auntie Ann disciplined me, like the former sergeant she was, and starting at an early age. If my clothes weren't rolled up in a certain way, my drawers got dumped and I started over again. She was a tough old bird. If I left a dirty dish or pan in the sink and went to bed without cleaning up, I would be awakened by a smack on the head with the dirty dish or pan I left in the sink. After a few lumps, I learned that I'd better clean up after myself. They didn't let me get away with anything. Both my aunt and my mom were amazing women, not just good-hearted, but very creative problem solvers and completely self-sufficient. How many people can say that?

And something else happened that I'll never forget. Most kids were listening to rock 'n' roll in the 1950s and very early 60s. Interestingly, I had a passion for classical music and opera. Auntie Ann had a collection of old records—78s of Tchaikovsky, Mahler, Beethoven, Chopin, and Brahms. When she went to work or when I thought she was otherwise occupied and wouldn't find me, I'd put the 78s on the record player and go lie on her bed to listen. She also had old 78s of Italian tenor Enrico Caruso, Russian basso profondo Feodor Chaliapin, and Italian baritone Tito Ruffa. In their day, in the 1920s, they were called the triumvirate (after Roman Emperors) because they were the three best in all opera in their vocal ranges.

I listened to Caruso sing all of his famous arias. I listened to Ruffa sing something called triple-tongue 32nd notes! I didn't care for the big choral groups or the operatic productions, but I loved the individual human voice in a solo. The craft, the beauty, and the artfulness of the instrument of the human voice were just a miracle to me. And my appreciation through the years has only deepened. When it's fully trained, the human voice is the most beautiful instrument in the world —all other instruments are mere attempts to copy the vibration of the human voice!

Years later, I found out that Auntie Ann knew I had listened to her 78s while she was out. She told me she knew because I hadn't pulled the bedcovers straight, and I left the imprint of my body on the bed. Sometimes I left the top of the record player open. It was harmless, so at the time I was listening, she didn't say anything to stop me from enjoying the music.

Unfortunately my Auntie Ann died from a heart attack at the early age of fifty-four. The result of her tough life, perhaps. She was working at the Flamingo Hotel as a waitress in the show room when she passed. I really missed her.

Time with My Father

At fourteen years old, and about to be a high school sophomore, I went to live with my Dad for a while. My mother got hold of him and said, "Your children should know who their father is. Why don't you have them up for the summer?" He said OK. He was remarried at the time. It was my first ride on a jet plane, a 707 from Las Vegas to Chicago. Jolene and I landed at O'Hare airport.

My father and his wife, Maureen, picked us up in a convertible—a dark blue Mercury, as I recall. They lived in McHenry, Illinois, not too far from Chicago. He worked in the city; he was president of International Chemical Company. It was not a huge, prestigious company, but good-sized. My father was a brilliant man, basically a research chemist by inclination. He had worked his way up in the corporate world and owned a beautiful home on the Fox River. He owned a speedboat, a cruiser, his own dock, and a Volkswagen Karmann Ghia, too. It had something wrong with the muffler and it sounded like a B-29 bomber—I loved it!

My father was a kind man who could tell jokes spontaneously. We spent a lot of time together as we had fourteen years to catch up on in just a few months.

Both my dad and Maureen were avid readers. Evenings were mostly spent sitting in the living room with our books.

I remember playing a game with my father where I would take one of his big Webster's world dictionaries and look up the goofiest, longest, most convoluted words I could find. I would just flip pages and find one bizarre word after another. I would read one of the words to my father. First of all, he would correct my pronunciation. Then he would spell it. Then he would give me the literal dictionary definition and how to use it in a sentence. I never stumped him. Not once. For some reason, that just impressed the hell out of me.

His master's degrees were in English and chemistry. He didn't go for a Ph.D., but he was just a brilliant, brilliant man with a rated IQ of 185, which is super genius level. And he was very spiritual in his own way. He wasn't religious, but spiritual, I would say.

I think that possibly at the age of fourteen, in talking with my father, my world view of humanity and spirituality began to take shape. To me, spirituality is the underpinning of all religious expression—the ground state, the common base from which all religious expressions are derived. My father showed me how things fit together, that different religions were the expression of a society or a culture or a climate or a particular style of living. He demonstrated how they are neither good nor bad, but simply appropriate for that place, time, people, and culture.

I was taught not to be bigoted or narrow-minded or look at things from only one direction, because there is so much that we miss when we close our minds. My father taught me to keep my mind open and not to be judgmental. You can learn something from everything and everyone. It all fits together if you look at life as a huge and beautiful tapestry where every thread has its place.

In that regard, he was one of my great teachers who began to give me a worldview of understanding, of openness, of willingness to learn and to look for the truth and beauty in something, rather than to look for what's wrong.

When we look for what's wrong, we're usually in a judgmental mode, based on what someone has told us about what's right or wrong or from what we've read, rather than from personal experience and what's in front of our own eyes. When we remove the blinders of narrow-minded conditioning, we see a much wider world and with an open mind, we learn.

My father taught me the scientific method and how it applies to the principles of life. There are steps in scientific thinking where you start with hypothesis and wind up with a law. It's always based upon experiment, observation, repeating the experiment, keeping an open mind, and revising your hypothesis until you find something that is repeatable and the result becomes predictable. It works in all circumstances. To me, life is like that. Life is a big experiment.

Rather than taking a dogma or a doctrine and saying, "This is truth," I learned to say, "This is someone's understanding of truth based upon…." Then I'd take a look at where this understanding came from. What were the conditions under which they were taught? What were the family environment, the cultural environment, the natural environment, and the social and political influences? All these contribute to thoughts, to ideas and beliefs, not just to religion, but also to politics and sociology and economics. All these interacting conditions form the mental framework of what someone believes is true or not true. Lastly, and most importantly, does this truth or concept work for them; does it make them happy or feel good? If so, then it is a valid truth for them. In this context, "truth" is a mental concept conditioned by many internal and external factors in a constant state of flux.

Hence, I became interested in anthropology—the origins of civilizations and cultures and what drives them. How do all the pieces of the cultural puzzle fit together to form the basis for the different belief systems around the world?

From my father's contribution to my learning, today I can say the following regarding religions or any personal belief systems:

Truth is what is working for and within people's lives so that they are reasonably happy, in harmony with others and their environment.

From a socio-psychological perspective, untruth is a biased overlay of limited conceptual thinking onto someone else's personal truth—rationalizing and distorting it with opinions, doctrines, dogmas, and narrow-mindedness. By projecting that supposed "truth" onto another, it makes that person wrong and causes disharmony, strife, and suffering.

From this perspective, if someone or something is made right at the expense of someone or something else being made wrong, this is untruth (just this guy's opinion). Rather than projecting our own insecurities, our own culture, our own class distinctions, our own fears and limitations upon others, we can be open to possibilities, and open to learning without fear.

That is what my father taught me.

I Decide To Stay

I decided to stay with my father a while longer and started my sophomore year at McHenry High School. My sister decided to go live with our Aunt Mary, my mother's sister, in Hammond, Indiana, and go to high school there. I went out for football. I was skinny, I was light, and I'd get the crap pounded out of me. Though I was a fairly quick runner, I had to wear all kinds of protective padding. I very quickly realized that football was probably not a good career choice for me. I was too damned skinny and the football equipment weighed me down so much that it gave the behemoths a chance to catch up with me and squash me like a bug.

Ego Booster

On one occasion, the son of one of my father's friends asked me to spend the night at his house because his sister was having a slumber party. Eight very pretty little girls about my age were going to be running around the house in their nighties. You can imagine at the age of fourteen, with young hormones coursing through my body, this had the possibility to be very educational.

We were reading comics in his room. All of a sudden his sister came to the door and said, "Bob, would you please come outside for a minute?" We went out in the backyard. I swear on my soul, this is the truth. All seven of her girlfriends were lined up in a row. She said, "They all really like you. Every single one of them wants to go steady with you. Would you please pick one, and that's including me?" I picked this one tall girl whom I quite fancied. That was a very interesting experience. For a fourteen-year-old boy, going on fifteen, it was one of the most amazing experiences of my life. Definitely an ego booster.

Hospital Time

Shortly after that, sometime around October, I started feeling bad, a little off. My dad took me to the doctor and had some blood tests run. The next thing I knew, I was in the hospital. I had contracted infectious mononucleosis. They called it the kissing disease—go figure.

I had a number of girlfriends by then who were candy stripers (hospital volunteers). When they visited me, they brought me things I wasn't supposed to have. I had a regular black market going for me, plus all these pretty young things spending time in my room.

Days and days went by, then weeks. I spent my fifteenth birthday in the hospital. I began getting worse. I stopped eating. The doctor ordered intravenous feeding because I was losing too much weight. My mother came to visit me and came into my hospital room wearing a little mask—for Halloween. Naturally, she was very worried. It was then that I decided to go back to Las Vegas with her. My dad had his wife and his friends, and my sister was staying in Indiana with Aunt

47

Mary, my mother's sister. I just didn't want my Mom to be alone, though Auntie Ann still lived close to her.

Back to Las Vegas

Back in Las Vegas, I registered for high school to continue my education. During this time I went out with a lovely Jewish girl whose brother, Seth Lublin, was a very dear friend of mine. I used to spend days at a time with the Lublin family. I was the goyim (non-Jew) of the family.

I had the good fortune to participate with the family in their religious traditions. Based on my father's teachings, I was very open to learning new things of a spiritual nature. I was enchanted with the voice of the cantor at their synagogue. He had a phenomenally beautiful tenor voice. I learned about the Jewish faith, one more aspect of my evolving ecumenical background.

By this time, I was a junior in Las Vegas High School, and still didn't have a constant male figure from whom to learn how to be a guy. Growing up, I had been with women most of the time—my sister, mother, and aunt. So, for a time in high school, I started hanging out with the rough crowd to develop a male identity and persona, although I was never a violent or bad kid. That just wasn't in me. I did hang out with kids who had those tendencies, though. I started goofing off, cutting school, and getting beer and going out to Lake Mead and getting plastered. Nothing terrible, but I began hanging out with the wrong gang. I tried to play tough, but it wasn't me. Virtually all the guys I hung out with got sent to reform school. I didn't, but I came close.

Talk about stupid. One day I was with some of the guys, and I wanted to prove I was as cool and tough as they were. So there was a police car in a parking lot, and I tried to steal gas from it—naturally I got caught. I was sent down to Juvenile Home. My mother was at work when she got the call from the police. Meanwhile, at the detention facility, I locked myself in the bathroom because I knew she would kill me. I wouldn't let anybody in. Finally, I was released into her custody with no charges placed. Just a stupid kid stunt, and that was the end of my crime wave. I was not meant to be a criminal. I was too damned dumb. I got caught.

I went through high school as a mediocre student. It wasn't that I couldn't do the work. I had more fun hanging out with the guys. I never really studied and wound up with a C average.

One time my biology teacher said to me, "Bob, I know you can do better than this." I had failed one six-week grading period. "I'll bet you five dollars that you can't make an A in biology in the next grading period." OK, he got my attention and I said, "You've got yourself a bet!"

I pulled an A in the next grading period. I knew I could do it. I knew I had the genetic intelligence—just not the motivation.

By the way, something at this point must be said: My mother, as of this writing, is ninety-three, and probably the best human being I've ever met. The intelligence I got from my father, but any compassion, goodness, kindness, or generosity comes from my mother. I have never heard her say a harsh word about or to another human in her entire life—always a positive attitude, always trying to be helpful, and always loving. She is one of those rare souls who loves unconditionally, as naturally as you and I breathe. She is very religious (Roman Catholic), but she has never forced her beliefs down anyone's throat.

I consider myself incredibly fortunate to have someone like her in my life. Though I didn't have much in the world of material things or money, I was rich beyond measure in the really important values of love, compassion, and goodness. For that I'm always very thankful. My mother molded my character, and that you can't buy with any amount of money.

As a senior in high school, I was into industrial arts. I wasn't interested in science yet at that age. That came later. So I went into shop. That's what guys did when they had C averages. My teacher said I was pretty good working with a lathe and welding. I sort of had a knack for working with tools. What I found out later in life is that when I applied myself to anything, I was pretty good at it. At that point, I was still learning that truth about myself, so what happened next was important to awakening my possibilities. My shop teacher said, "You know, we ought to do something that nobody's ever done before for the State Industrial Arts contest"

That caught my attention.

"Let's make a gasoline engine from scratch, from bars of steel," he said.

"OK, that's neat," I said, with a very large question mark hanging above my head.

The next thing out of my mouth was, "I'm going to need a lot of help here."

Of course, he was more than willing to help, but he said that I had to do the work; those were the rules. It was going to be a one-cylinder engine—gasoline, water-cooled, with a crank shaft, a spark plug, a coil to give spark to the spark plug, a carburetor, a tank of water that cooled by convection through a water jacket welded around the cylinder, and a flywheel. WOW!

Go figure. Here's a sixteen-year-old kid working on a lathe with tolerances that had to be precise to 1/10,000 of an inch. I remember boring the cylinder and my teacher telling me, "Bob, don't mess this up. That cylinder wall has to be exact.

I had calipers that would stretch out and measure the diameter of the inside of the cylinder down to 10,000th of an inch. In the end I was taking metal off so fine with a tool bit from the lathe—so sharp you could shave with it—that all you could see was a fine powder coming off rather than a coil of steel. I was sweating bullets. I figured all I would have to do was hiccup and that bit would hit the side of the cylinder wall and about 500 hours of work would be down the drain! Then we had to bore ten cooling fins into the cylinder, which started out as a solid bar of steel. Those cooling fins had to be a certain width and depth but not hit the inside of the cylinder wall. One small little mistake boring into the side of another cooling fin or into the cylinder wall, and then there would be 800 hours down the drain! I almost had a nervous breakdown.

I cast my own piston out of melted aluminum. Then I turned it on a lathe. I made my own crankshaft and my own piston rod pin that rode on the piston, a flywheel, and cylinder casing and threads on the end of the cylinder that screwed into the housing where the crankshaft was. I was a kid, but I was doing what I would call master's level machinist work.

I have to admit that I did not silver solder the cooling jacket onto the cylinder. My teacher did that for me. I had gone so far and he didn't want me to screw it up late in the game, so he said he wanted to help me a little bit. The rest of it was mine.

Then we had it chromed and had a mahogany base made for it. We got a one-gallon gas can and placed pipes at the top and bottom. Red hoses (one that went into the top of the cylinder and one at the bottom) were attached to the pipes. The engine cooled by convection—hot water came out the top and pulled the cold water in from the bottom. The engine had a little spark plug. We got a car coil and chromed it.

We had a little pull starter, like on a lawn mower. You put a cord around the front of this little pulley where you have a knot that goes behind a notch, and just yank it. Be darned if it didn't start up on the first pull! The darn thing was cranking one horsepower at 10,000 rpm. It sounded like a little lawn mower on steroids. I was astounded.

We submitted it to the contest, and, lo and behold, I won second place in the state. The guy who won first place had a punch press accurate to 10,000[th] of an inch. OK. Big deal. My cylinder wall had to have that, much less the rest of the engine! So we were a little disappointed that I didn't take first.

A Marine's Life for Me

Right around the time I made the engine, when I would go for lunch, I would walk by the Marine Corps recruiting office near the high school. Good place for a recruiting office, I guess. I had always been captivated by the mystique of the Marines: the uniform, the warrior persona, first to fight, and all that kind of stuff. Here again, I was always trying to prove myself, fit myself into the male mold. The only male role models I had in Las Vegas were the tough kids at school, and most of them were in jail by then. So, a close friend of mine, Mike Bernhard, and I decided we were going into the Marines.

My recruiter was standing next to me in the *Las Vegas Sun* newspaper photo of me in suit and tie when I won the state contest for the engine I built in shop class. I'll never forget him. His name was Staff Sergeant Chuck Swindell. I used to go over to his office and help him send out bulk mailings to prospects. He would tell me stories of his time in the Marine Corps and show me literature.

Before I graduated high school, I actually joined the Marines. It was called the 120-day delay plan. I was in the active reserves. I went to Los Angeles along with my buddy and a couple of other guys from Las Vegas and was sworn in. By the way, Mike and I were separated after boot camp. He went to electronics school, but he also wound up in Vietnam, though I had already moved to the helicopter squadron by the time he arrived.

After our swearing in, I came back and finished my last few months of high school. I graduated in June 1964. In July I was on the bus headed for the Marine Corps Recruit Depot in San Diego, California, the beginning of a very eventful journey far beyond my wildest dreams and imaginings.

Bob and his mom, just after Boot Camp.

CHAPTER FOUR

The Man Who Moves On

The spiritual dimension of culture is not an array of dogmatic world views bristling with contradictions but a spectrum of contemplative practices, equivalent in essence, which lead toward experience rather than toward doctrinal assertion. — from *Coming Home: The Experience of Enlightenment in Sacred Traditions*, a book by poet and philosopher Lex Hixon (1941–1995)

And so I fought in Vietnam for almost two years. I was lucky enough to come back with all the important bits and pieces still intact. Somehow, the most "strategic territory" of my inner self was held sacred, even in the midst of combat. It was in Vietnam that I started a lifetime journey of balancing war and peace—most especially in my interior life where terrible demons and beautiful angels coexisted.

During my first tour in Vietnam, I remember asking the essential questions: Is this all life is? Is life nothing more than insanity and killing and hardship? Is this all that I am? Who am I? What is all this about? Why is there so much suffering in life? What are the things that cause us to do the things we do and feel? Why are we here in the first place?

We find out what we are really made of when we come face to face with the insanity of war and stare death straight in the eye. I had lived, fought, and worked under the most primitive conditions you can imagine. Like waiting for an enemy attack in the middle of the night in a fighting hole filled with two feet of water from the torrential downpours of monsoon season; and taking "showers" standing in those same hard rains to wash some of the crud off. Sleeping next to a swamp that bred huge mosquitoes; eating C-rations canned before I was born; and drinking out of the "water buffalo," which was nothing but a big green tank with a spigot on wheels.

Perhaps my questioning came from the surreal situation that was playing itself out around me. I think anyone would begin some form of inner questioning, even as simple as, "What in the world am I doing here?" My questioning just took a little different turn.

I wrote home and asked my mother and sister to send me some books on philosophy. I thought maybe in philosophy there would be something to give me a handle on why humans seem almost compelled toward continuous conflict, like war, and how I fit into this madness?

I got the *Dialogues* of Plato, and the works of Heidegger, Kant, and Schopenhauer. However, I gravitated to Immanuel Kant more than to anyone else, because I felt he had a more spiritual approach to philosophy. These existential philosophers were very interesting and intellectual, with very nice rationalizations, but they didn't answer any questions. I discovered that philosophy doesn't answer questions. It just asks more questions.

I read for four or five months, and then I stopped, because Western philosophy simply went in circles using big words that left my big questions unanswered. Even though I had temporarily stopped my philosophical pursuits, the questions still lingered like an itch I could not scratch. Every now and again some thoughts would surface: This makes no sense. This is goofy. Humans have to be put here for a little bit higher purpose than to figure out more and creative ways to destroy each other!

56

It was somewhat frustrating, I guess, that I didn't find answers right away, but it forced me into a mode of continual inquiry, to at least look for answers and be open to all possibilities. I didn't have any preconceptions, no fixed concepts of what life and reality and people should be. I realized that when you don't know and you admit you don't know, and don't have the answers, then you are open for the answers to come to you in one form or another.

Sometimes I got flashes, or inklings, in conversations or situations where I would see—in the midst of chaos and the craziness of war— acts of kindness, caring, and love that happened spontaneously, right alongside, and coexistent with, the insanity of trying to blow each other up. It was a paradox. How could such polar opposites exist together in the same time, in the same place, within the same people? Again, more questions. Not very many answers at that point, but it started me doing more questioning.

The questions lay dormant until I got out of the Marine Corps on July 1, 1968. I had served four years and four months of duty, honoring and protecting my country.

When I got back to Las Vegas, it was the summer of 1968 and I was twenty-one years old. I realized very quickly that there wasn't much of a market for a door gunner or somebody who could sling explosives around. So I thought about joining the police force, which many Marines did, or going to school to earn a degree in criminal law and then getting a job in the sheriff's department.

The only school near my house was Southern Nevada Technical Center. I thought I'd drop by and see what was going on. I walked in the front door and, off to my right, a lot of racket was coming out of this one room. I looked in, and there was this little guy with two big decks of 80-column punched cards in his hands, all this equipment making noise, cards moving, paper moving, and lights flashing.

I go, "What is this?"

"It's called data processing," he replied.

"Yeah? Wow. This looks pretty cool!"

We talked and I enlisted, or rather, I enrolled in a two-year degree program called Electronic Data Processing, which included English, accounting, and many other business courses as well. I worked nights at McCarran Field, parking and fueling airplanes at the private airport. My first class was at 7:30 in the morning. I would strip off my overalls, take a shower, clean up, put on a suit and tie, and pick up a briefcase and my glasses. That's how I would go to school every day. I thought, if you want to be successful you had to look successful—it's an attitude thing.

I studied very hard, did extra credit work for the school district, and assisted in teaching material that I had just learned. I took tests only for the first semester in data processing. After that, I didn't take another test in that course for the rest of my time in school. Rather, the instructor had me compose the tests for the rest of the class to take. No, it did not come easily to me; I had to study six hours a day and work twice as hard as everybody else to pull off A's in almost all my subjects. I was back to getting two or three hours of sleep a night and, damn, it felt like I was back in the Corps.

Home Is Not a Place

When I got out of the Corps, I was basically a nervous wreck. Then I took on the pressure and stress of finding a career that I could make money at. Add to that my being a high achiever in school during the day and working at night. Yes, it was just like being back in Vietnam—the only difference was no one was shooting at me. I had the GI Bill, but I still had to work full time to pay my way through school. Getting an average of three hours of sleep per night, I was literally burning myself out.

A dear friend's mother, Della Bernhard, was a teacher of Transcendental Meditation (TM). I always thought she was a little on the goofy side, but I loved her very much. Because I grew up as much in her house with Mike as I did in my own home, she was like a second mom. One day she told me, "Come in here, sit down, shut up, do what I tell you, and when we're finished you can ask questions." She taught me how to meditate using TM. It was probably the first time in my life I had ever begun to shut down some of the outer noise and internal mind chatter. I wasn't conscious immediately of making the shift from noise to silence—it was a gradual process. But TM was for me a unique and profound experience, another step on the journey home.

I learned that many different techniques of meditation practice required thinking about something or focusing on an object, but that those forms keep the mind on the surface level and engaged. TM allowed my mind to settle down into a quiet state where thought disappeared, but awareness remained. This was my first experience of a deeper state of consciousness within myself.

I dutifully meditated twice a day for twenty minutes. I gradually felt some of my stress ease off. I was able to keep my grades up and keep working. I was more relaxed, happier, more at peace.

The interesting thing was that I had always been looking for a place in the world or out of it where I fit, some place to call home—as a boy looking for the spaceship in our backyard in Florida or in the middle of the desert near Las Vegas. Meditation was the first time that I had a faint glimmer of the fact that home was not a place and that maybe I should look for home on the inside, not the outside. It was the first time there was a glimmering of that idea. I didn't articulate it in those specific words at that time, but there was a sense that there's more here than meets the eye, because I felt somewhat different than before. I felt more peaceful, more integrated, less fragmented. Concentration came easier.

Digging Deeper into Esoteric Origins

I started to study Eastern philosophy and the more esoteric aspects of the major religions, the mystic portions. I was operating from the groundwork laid when I had stayed with my father and which continued when I was studying philosophy in Vietnam. I wanted to understand foundations of the human condition. What were the visions of those who founded the major religions? What were they really saying? Were they saying, "Put me up on a pedestal," "Deify me"? Or perhaps they were saying, "Look within yourself and you can do anything I can do. There's no difference between you and me other than that I took the trouble to find where home was, and you can do the same."

I learned from digging into the depths of the various major world religions—Buddhism, Christianity, Judaism, Islam—that at their roots they all say the same thing. It's like pearls on a string. Each religion is a pearl, each one an expression of fundamental truth and not in any way in conflict with each other or any other expression of fundamental truth. There is only One Truth, in essence, appearing as many in form.

These are the things I found for myself as I began to get more in touch with that active silence within me. Not words, not concepts, not a belief system. It was direct experience of something very quiet, but that quietness had characteristics of wholeness and awareness without content. It wasn't blank. It was lively, but silent. It was like one fountain from which all streams of water flow down the mountain. It was the same water just taking different paths. The fountainhead of life—Home!

I never had any problems reading any particular philosophical or religious scripture, because I could see behind the words to what was really being said. I saw no conflict. Nobody had to be better. Nobody had to have the only "truth." It was all truth, but seen from different angles, like facets of a diamond. It's only from insecurity in our own

60

beliefs that we say, "Our guy or gal is better than your guy or gal. If ours is better and yours is not as good, then I win." That made no sense to me whatsoever. We are humanity, made of the same stuff. We come from different parts of the planet, different cultures and climates, different economic structures and political systems; but ultimately, we are all humankind. Our basic foundation is the same. We are different expressions of the same human condition. It's only when we believe that one expression is better or worse or higher or lower than another that the problems start.

I learned that we are not Catholics or Protestants or Jews. We are humankind and live the same "Ultimate Truth" in all its diversity.

My esoteric studies helped me further develop the sense that anyone can believe exactly as they so choose—that is their freedom. It was not up to me to say you are right or wrong or anything else. The only person I had a right to do or say anything about was myself.

A Tiny Hole in a Black Wall

I graduated from technical school a semester early with a 3.7 grade point average. (second-year typing class pulled it down). In a class of forty-two, I was number two—I missed number one by a hair's breadth. That's not too bad, I suppose. I learned to live with that one.

At the time, two businessmen were developing a software company, and they wanted to hire the top two grads to get it started. I began work as a programmer, then became an analyst. Eventually I was put in charge of marketing and sales and designing systems and programming. I had a territory of four states—Nevada, Utah, Arizona, and California—which required considerable driving. This all happened only a year out of school.

During this time, I continued my twice-a-day TM practice. One interesting observation that I have made over the years is that there has always been a tremendous parallel between my outer life and my inner or spiritual life. We are one whole entity; what affects one part of us affects the entire being. As understanding unfolds from within, more of our latent mental potential becomes activated, and the more we use it, the more we get. Of course, I see this only in retrospect because at the time I was just trying to get through each day with a minimum of screw-ups.

In the early days of my meditation practice, it was almost like there was a black wall inside of me, and when I would meditate, there was a tiny hole that began to appear in the black wall. As I meditated over the months and years, this hole got bigger a little at a time. It's not that there was something on the other side of the wall that was in physical form, but a sense of openness, a sense of not being as walled off from that part of my inner self as I was before. I wanted to know more about that. I found it a very interesting experience.

What became very apparent to me as I continued to practice TM meditation was that my mind was incredibly stuck on a superficial level, a very narrow band of thought process. The only thing I got from my TM meditation, at first, was the understanding of how stuck my mind was—like a fly in amber. I guess the first step in changing is to recognize the need for change. The more I meditated, the more this tiny hole in the opaqueness of my mind began to expand.

While I was continuing to meditate, I read *The Science of Being and the Art of Living: Transcendental Meditation* by Maharishi Mahesh Yogi. He talked about the inner self, this sense of being, of I am-ness, that there is the observer, the perceiver of the thoughts that happen within the mind, and the perceiver of sensations as input from the bodily senses.

I began to be aware of this silent observer more and more deeply.

I told Della, my TM teacher and second mom, that I wanted to know more, to become a teacher of TM, and to spend some time with

Maharishi Mahesh Yogi. For two years, I gave her fifty dollars a week out of my paycheck, and she held it for me. By 1971, I had enough money so that Della could sign me up for a five-month training course with Maharishi on the island of Majorca, Spain, in the middle of the Mediterranean Sea.

I turned in my resignation at work. I sold my car. I put my clothes in a pack on my back, and I jumped on a plane.

CHAPTER FIVE

Seeking That Which Does Not Change

The modern hero, the modern individual who dares to heed the
call and seek the mansion of that presence with whom
it is our whole destiny to be atoned, cannot, indeed must
not, wait for his community to cast off its slough of
pride, fear, rationalized avarice, and sanctified
misunderstanding.... It is not society that is to guide and
save the creative hero, but precisely the reverse. And so
every one of us shares the supreme ordeal—carries the
cross of the redeemer—not in the bright moments of his
tribe's great victories, but in the silences of his personal
despair. — Joseph Campbell, American author and teacher of
comparative mythology, in his book *The Hero with a Thousand
Faces* (1968)

Transcendental Meditation is based on the 3,500-year-old
tradition of self-realization that originated in India. The
knowledge has been handed down by Vedic masters from
generation to generation for thousands of years. Maharishi established
it in the West in the 1960s.

When I arrived on the island of Majorca, I discovered that
Maharishi had rented maybe six or eight hotels. In those days, he was

trying some experiments in consciousness, in expanding people's awareness, and looking at their experiences with different levels of consciousness, which he called Cosmic Consciousness, God Consciousness, and Unity Consciousness. Please don't ask me to define these, as I could never understand the supposed subtle differences among them. As usual, I simplified things for myself. There is silent awareness and there is the content within awareness. One is never changing, the other ever changing. That is as far as I could perceive it.

Exploring these levels of consciousness meant that Maharishi was having people engage in meditations alternating with sessions of yoga postures for many, many hours a day. Naturally, being who I am, I always go for the most extreme measure of anything possible. Within a few weeks, I was meditating almost eighteen hours per day. One meditation might be five or six hours. I would sit down, close my eyes, and there was a sense of awareness, but no fidgeting. My bodily functions, my whole metabolism, slowed down to a crawl. I experienced tremendously deep rest and silence, but I was not asleep.

The hole in the black wall of my mind kept getting bigger and bigger. That was kind of interesting for me, and rather exciting, because I wanted to know what was on the other side of the wall. This constant search for home, I'd realized, was not a place outside of me. Home was on the other side of that wall, or within myself. All the running that I'd been doing here and there, trying desperately to find what I was, who I was, where I fit in, was driven by some force from within, and it would not stop pushing me.

Every single human being asks these questions to one degree or another, and most of us are looking in the wrong direction for answers. The answers do not come from any place, person, or concept, but from within ourselves—everything else is second-hand knowledge accumulated from books, other people, or society. Only direct experience of our Source, that quiet, steady, pure awareness within ourselves, will truly satisfy our yearning for the truth and answer all of these identity questions.

In deep meditation, the mind begins to settle down, thoughts become more tenuous, less defined, as the energies of the mind settle into a state of equilibrium—silence. The witnessing factor (awareness without content) begins to shine through to the mind more clearly because it is not obstructed by all the noise of continual mental activity.

This is a state of deep peace to the mind and deep rest to the body: a state of wholeness and well-being. All we are doing is permeating the entirety of the mind with that energy of balance and peace. Some of that energy "sticks" when we come out into normal daily activity—we are more energetic, creative, and loving, as that is the nature of that energy. But it's not instant pudding. We have a lot of nonsense accumulated within the mind, and it is only by repeated exposure to the source of pure, unblemished energy that the junk within the mind slowly but surely dissolves and evaporates; like on a hot day, ice turns to water and the water evaporates into the air.

This level of prolonged deep meditation is not normal for westerners. It is a very unusual condition within the mind and nervous system, and many people at Maharishi's teacher training course, honestly, went over the edge of the cliff with no parachute (psychotic). A special group took care of the people who went twitchy and disassociated with outer reality, as we all know and love it. This was a great example of taking a good thing to an unhealthy extreme. BALANCE—between activity and silence—is the key, not meditating eighteen hours a day. When I felt myself getting twitchy or shaky inside, I had a unique way of re-grounding myself.

This was during the winter of 1972, right on the cliffs of the Mediterranean Sea. There was a 150-foot cliff, like a seawall, where the hotel was. It was pretty chilly, and the Mediterranean was very choppy with waves. The water was ice cold. The waves would crash up against the cliff and just race up the wall at about 150 miles per hour, sending a deluge of water over the top of the cliff and over the little sea wall that was about three feet high and kept people from falling over the cliff. I would get my swim trunks on, walk out to the seawall, put my hands on the bricks of the seawall, grab hold, and lean over. Watching these huge waves, with hundreds of thousands of tons of water racing up at me, was breathtaking.

I would almost disappear in these ice-cold waves of water from the Mediterranean. Then, after ten or fifteen minutes, I'd shake myself off, turn around, go back inside, dry off, have breakfast, and everything was locked back into place again. I did it once a week and everything was fine.

I did the long meditations for three-and-a-half months, and then tapered it down as we began to learn the techniques of TM teacher training. It was rigorous, harder than learning computers and programming. We had to memorize a lot of techniques, understand all the variables that were possible in a meditation setting, and learn ways of answering all kinds of questions students could raise.

Scruffy Nerf Herder with Tattoos

I met my future wife, Laura Viernstein, at the course in Majorca. From the window in the hotel dining room, she had a panoramic view of my somewhat odd routine of challenging the waves.

Laura had graduated with a master's in psychology from Wake Forest University in Winston-Salem, North Carolina. She was working at University of North Carolina, Chapel Hill Medical School before arriving for TM training in Majorca. She was upper middle class America. Her father was a biomedical engineer for Johns Hopkins Applied Physics Laboratory and Medical School, and her mother

67

was a musician and teacher. Laura's brother, Karl, was in seminary to become a Presbyterian minister. She came from a brilliant family.

By comparison, I was like a scruffy "nerf herder," to quote Princess Leia to Han Solo in the movie *Star Wars*. A lot of guys in the course were trying to be the gentle, soft-spoken meditation teachers in suits and ties. But I wasn't trying to be anything but myself. I was running around in Levis, flannel shirt, and tire-tread sandals. I stood out like a sore thumb. And then there were the two rather large tattoos on my upper arms. On my left arm was an image of the eagle, globe, and anchor of the Marine Corps, with the words "Death Before Dishonor." It was a classic. On my right arm was a naked lady—she had nice boobs, good ass, and long hair. In Vietnam it became a tradition for guys to pat the butt of the tattooed girl on my arm for good luck before flying a combat mission. Marines don't do love pats! They'd give me a stiff whack, though in a friendly way.

As you might imagine in a meditation course, with everyone trying to be ever so spiritual, my tattoos went over like a fart in a space suit. I never was good at playing social games—made my skin itch.

Silence Is As Silence Does

As a fairly new out-of-the-Corps Marine, I naturally tended to vocalize just exactly what I was thinking. This manifested itself one day in Maharishi's course in Majorca. Some of the course participants decided that we were going to have three days of silence. I could get along with that; I had no problem. But when we were sitting down for breakfast, people were making all of these hand and facial gestures trying to communicate with each other. All this gesturing nonsense was to me the antithesis of silence. They simply replaced the sound of speech with face and hand motions. That was not silence.

I thought that was so disingenuous, and I wasn't going to have any part of it. I got fed up. I was sitting there slowly seething, having some eggs or something. When my internal thermometer hit the boiling point, I said in my best Marine Corps drill instructor voice, "Would somebody please pass me the fucking salt?" You could have heard a pin drop. There were 300 people in the dining room. It was like I had thrown a hand grenade in a cathedral with the Pope. They were horrified, first of all that I would talk, secondly that I would do it very loud, and thirdly, that I would use somewhat strong language. People were just aghast. They looked at me like, "How dare you?" And I just sat there daring anyone to say anything. I looked at them like, "Go ahead, assholes—make my day."

We went to the lecture hall that evening to listen to Maharishi. More than 700 people were in the room, but as soon as Maharishi came in and sat down, about ten people right in the front rows raised their hands. They couldn't wait to tell on the scruffy nerf herder.

"Maharishi! Maharishi!"

And Maharishi said, "Yes, what is it?"

"Maharishi, we had three days of silence and this one guy was talking and speaking loudly in the cafeteria."

Maharishi looked at them and said, "If you want to be silent, just be silent."

And I'm thinking, "YES! You jerks."

It was the most practical thing—if you want to be quiet, just don't talk. Don't try to impose your will on someone else. I mean, there were those who talked quietly in their own sections. And, if you didn't want to hear somebody talk, then you could sit elsewhere and everybody would be happy. But don't try to impose some artificial personal agenda on others.

You can imagine I wasn't one of the most popular people there. Laura did not seem to be horrified with my being a little rough around the edges. OK, ok—*a lot* rough around the edges!

After five months, I became a TM teacher and returned to Las Vegas. Maharishi asked Laura to go with him to Italy to put together some advanced training courses. I would call her from Las Vegas, and it was costing me a small fortune. Finally one day I said, "I can't afford all these long distance international phone calls. It would be much easier if we just got married." Funnily enough, she agreed.

On June 10, 1972, we were married in Bethesda, Maryland, and she moved from the lovely Washington, D.C., area to the middle of the desert outside of Las Vegas with me. I'm not sure she really knew what she was getting into.

After about three months of job-hunting, I got a good job as an analyst/programmer for the Las Vegas Valley Water District, and Laura was hired as the psychologist for Opportunity Village Association for Retarded Citizens in Las Vegas. A very good start to our marriage.

CHAPTER SIX

Singing As We Go

Why not go forward singing all the way? It makes the going
easier. — from *The Eclogues*, Book IX, the pastoral poems of Virgil
(70 B.C.-19 B.C), the Roman poet best known for writing *The Aeneid*

Laura and I settled into the good life. Our daughters, Colleen
and Crystal, were born in Las Vegas in the first years of our
marriage. We continued to practice and teach TM.

Life, quite literally, was singing our song.

Both Laura and I had a history of singing. I had sung Gregorian
chant in the Catholic church in my boyhood. Laura sang in the church
choir throughout her youth and had studied voice at Queens University
in Charlotte, North Carolina.

We decided to take further voice training for fun. We found a voice
coach, Leonard Bushell, a tenor in the New York Metropolitan Opera,
who had retired and moved to Las Vegas. Both Laura and I signed
up for lessons. I went twice a week for two years; Laura went once
a week.

For the first year, I sang scales and vowel sounds. This practice
teaches you to relax the muscles in your face and throat that you are
not using for singing, and to use only the muscles that should be
working—around the vocal chords. What happens when most of us try
to sing is that we tighten the face and throat. This distorts the sound. In
the vocal exercises I learned to touch my face to be sure that it wasn't

tight as I made sounds. The less tight, the better the sound. It's really a good metaphor for life. The more we strain, the more difficult our task is, and we expend more energy than is necessary. In singing you have to be very relaxed—to sing a full repertoire, your voice has to last. You have to support the voice from the diaphragm, and hit the notes simply by tightening and loosening the vocal chords.

I had a hard time learning to relax, but eventually I graduated from scales to singing famous operatic baritone arias. I was good but not great. I stuck to computers, a wise decision in retrospect.

I sang in a couple of dinner clubs, and Laura and I sang duets in churches. We also sang Handel's *Messiah* with choral groups—we loved singing together.

Moving to Stelle, Illinois

In 1976 an opportunity came up for our family to become part of a private intentional community in Stelle, Illinois, 85 miles south of Chicago. It was self-contained, but not a new age community nor a hippie commune. It was comprised of individuals who valued self-reliance, striving for excellence, and nurturing a love for learning, life, and others. We thought it would be a good environment for us to raise the children. Stelle had lovely homes, and we picked out a four-bedroom, three-bath.

The community had its own manufacturing and water-producing facilities as well as a Montessori school. I wanted to see what it would be like to live cooperatively with other families, but in separate lives, and to help each other. For example, if there were kids around, you would help them just like you would your own kids.

So we moved to Illinois where I got a job as a manager of data processing for a leasing company. Laura took care of our children and our home and was active in the community.

After we moved, Laura and I continued our voice training, this time with a lovely woman named Ruth Marie Eimer who was on the faculty of Olivet Nazarene University. I took voice for another two years, so I had almost four years of classical training to sing opera. I learned the famous baritone roles such as "Prelude to Pagliacci" in Italian. I had grown up loving the great tenor voice of Enrico Caruso. But I longed to have the cavernous voice of Sherrill Milnes or Robert Merrill, both phenomenal Metropolitan Opera baritones. I never quite got to that level.

I had a good voice, but I did not have a great voice, nor the motivation to train to the degree necessary that I could make a living. That's a tough racket. I loved to sing and I learned to sing well—not for a career, but for my own enjoyment. I could break into song just about anywhere, much to the chagrin of my wife and my children when they grew old enough to be embarrassed. If we were in a crowd somewhere, my girls would look at me horrified. Other people would just stare and think, "He's fallen out of his tree."

Interestingly enough, vocal training taught me something very important. It showed me that you don't always have to work really hard at something to do it well. What I mean is that if you are focused and you are applying the proper techniques in anything you do, you are using energy very efficiently. But if you are forcing and straining, you distort the results and just get tired quickly. This concept transferred well to my career in information technology.

Although I started my career as an analyst/programmer and moved into work in sales and customer support, I found myself at Armour Pharmaceutical Company in Kankakee, Illinois, in 1977, managing a whole department. I was responsible for processing all information necessary to make life-critical drugs like insulin, thyroid medication, and human blood expander. I worked very hard, so when Revlon Corporation bought Armour from Greyhound later that year, I found myself rising quickly to the position of division director of the prescription pharmaceuticals product group, five companies within the Revlon Health Care Group.

I was well known as the "guy who could get things done" all the way up to the board room of Revlon. "If you need to accomplish something critical in IT on time and within budget, go see that guy in Kankakee, Illinois, and he'll get it done!"

As in learning to sing and perform, I focused. I learned the proper techniques, and I got things done with the efficient use of energy.

Common Religious Ground

I was still very ecumenical—Catholic, Protestant, Jewish, Hindu, Buddhist, and more—deepening my understanding. We went to a Methodist church in Bourbonnais, Illinois, near where I worked. I enjoyed cooking at the men's breakfast and helping out at the church. I became acquainted with our minister, whom I liked very much. He never tried to say this is good or that is bad. He gave his congregation workable ideas that could help them in their lives. I wanted to get more involved in the church without going to seminary for years. His response was that I should become a lay minister. To get certified I had to make the three-hour drive one way to Peoria, Illinois, for eight weekends. For a time, I wrote and delivered sermons for services when area ministers went on vacation.

There was no conflict between my meditation practice and Christian religion, or the teachings of Jesus. "I and my Father are one" (John 10:30) was completely in line with my personal experience during meditation. It seemed easy for us to look literally at religious or theological works that great people had written, but for me it was essential to look more deeply into the meaning of the words in light of my personal experience.

74

I believe when Jesus said, "I am the way, the truth, and the life: no man cometh unto the Father, but by me" (John 14: 6) that He was referring to that Christ consciousness within Him and all of us, not exclusively to his personhood as Jesus of Nazareth. I believe He was saying that you can't get to that absolute love, the greatest expression of the divine impulse, unless it is through the human condition; unless it is within yourself that you find it as He and others had done. Granted, that is my interpretation, but what the heck…it still works for me today.

Even now, I do not debate my theological position with anyone; what is important is how I treat others and how I live my life by the principles of love and compassion that Jesus taught. To me, theological arguments are a complete waste of time because they are just head stuff having nothing to do with how you live your life. Living the principles Jesus taught is what is important, and not contemplating complex theologies like how many angels can dance on the head of a pin (pick your own theological discussion).

I can go to the Methodist church, a synagogue, a Baptist church, or a Buddhist temple and see beyond the trappings of the doctrines, dogmas, buildings, paintings, and icons, to the foundation of what the original founders were trying to give to the people. It is the understanding that within each person is a field of completeness, a core of energy that is joy and unconditional love. And we're all connected to each other and the universe by that energy, that love.

This period of study and reflection as a lay minister refined my concept of the common spiritual ground that various peoples of the world share.

I could never believe that any power in charge of the diversity of creation could ever make a one-only religion and declare it the best one and that every other religion was secondary and not as good. Logically it didn't make any sense. If everyone says, "My religion is the best," well, then, as they used to say on that TV show *To Tell the Truth*, "Would the real religion please stand up?" What is the point? Does everybody else have to be wrong for me to be right? Doesn't it seem more reasonable that in a world of more than seven billion people that there is something for everyone? This to me would be the true divine expression of love and compassion, where nobody gets left out! A God of true compassion, love, and wisdom would have all the mechanisms in place so that at any particular point in time every individual would get what is right for them, giving them hope and meaning in life. Is that not the true definition of compassion, love, and wisdom? Why does something or somebody else have to be better?

I could never figure out the narrowness of mind that elevates one religion over another. And I still can't.

In my pursuit of spiritual truth during this period of my life, I probably did not articulate my insights in full detail, except, perhaps, in some of my lay sermons. But in my heart, I knew this simple truth: At our core all humanity is the same, divine in essential nature, but appearing in different forms. Not only all of humanity but all of creation is linked together through energy and consciousness. All of these apparent differences work together, exist together, in harmony together. Does the tree fight with the blade of grass? Does the cloud fight with the mountain? I certainly have not seen any gang wars in the forest recently—the Oak Gang against the Elm Gang. Yes, it sounds silly, and just as silly as when we do it.

The innumerable names, forms, ideas, and concepts are all part of the great tapestry of life. Why do any person's beliefs have to be right or wrong? If it were wrong, it could not exist. I don't believe the universe creates wrongness. The outward expression may not be life-supporting, may be distorted, so we have wars and uprisings in the name of religion or ideology. But it's not religion that is wrong—it's that our animal brain is not yet sophisticated enough to cognize the link between the outward manifestation or expression of a philosophy of life and the inner Truth that is underlying that expression. So we have these incredible wars and arguments over "God" for nothing. The difference is in the words only; the underlying principle is the same "One" existence.

The common denominator I have found in all of life and within the core of all religions is love—a spontaneous upwelling, a fullness and wholeness from within. Love is not necessarily words or thoughts, but is a profound unifying feeling that is trying to express itself in all aspects of our lives. Regardless of what is happening all around us, that completeness is unshakable. You could say that Love equals God. This Love/God allows all the different expressions of life to live in harmony if we just give them the opportunity—prayer and meditation are ways of doing this.

As long as we try to deepen our experience of that unifying principle, then we can live within all this diversity in peace and harmony. We can stop fighting and stop trying to figure out who is better or what is best.

The expression of this unconditional love does not mean tolerance. I believe that tolerance is often just anger suppressed and pushed into the background. With true unconditional love, there is a spontaneous and clear understanding and acceptance. That doesn't mean anything goes—the universe has its way of keeping things in balance.

Applying these insights, I began to learn that disharmony only occurred in my life when I tried to make the outside world fit my mental preconceptions. This realization helped me in every aspect of my life, but especially in my career.

As an executive, I wanted to develop the qualities of a good leader, not just a good manager. A leader inspires. A manager controls. Inspiring others comes from wisdom and understanding, so I cultivated compassion as the dominant focus of my leadership strategy. Yes, sometimes control is necessary, but it should not be the dominant focus.

Taking the Next Step

Living in the intentional community in Stelle was wonderful for the first year or so. But I had always found that anything really good has within itself the seeds of its own destruction. Somebody always tries to change things to fit their mold of right and good. In my view, the people in the community ceased to live the ideal I moved there for. So, rather than argue, Laura and I just left.

I continued to expand my understanding not so much of religion, but of the singular driving force in all of humanity: the quest to understand our place in the universe. Why are we here? On a deeply personal level, that question had always translated to "Where is my true home?" Admittedly, my understanding was still very much in my rational mind. Logic guided my process, but my powers of intuition and the very heart of me where all my yearnings gathered were about to come into their own.

Going to war, practicing TM, learning how to sing, studying religion, searching for home, working hard in my career to support my family—all these aspects of my life thus far were the perfect preamble, the perfect preparation, for the next major period of my life: friendship and study with Gururaj Ananda Yogi.

CHAPTER SEVEN

My Friend and Teacher: Gururaj Ananda Yogi

True friendship is to find Divinity in the friend. And as you find Divinity in the friend, you will find a subtle transformation taking place in the friend as well. You will find him being uplifted, and he will not know why. He will only respond by loving you more, and he will not know why he is loving you more. Meanwhile you are creating that love in his heart for you, because you have started loving him. And that is true friendship. — Gururaj Ananda Yogi

About eight months before we left the intentional community in Stelle, one of our former Transcendental Meditation students back in Las Vegas reconnected with us. She told us about a guru who offered individualized practices and who seemed to her to be the real deal.

Our friend wanted to give us Gururaj Ananda Yogi's preparatory meditation techniques. She knew that Laura and I were very much into TM—however, we were always open. Any time you close yourself off and say, "There is no other truth but this," then you shut yourself off from any other opportunities for knowledge and growth. The unknown manifests in unexpected ways, providing the opportunities for expansion of our personal horizons when we have an open mind and heart.

So, we said, "Sure."

Our friend's husband flew from Las Vegas to Chicago to Stelle to teach us the preparatory meditation techniques, and Laura and I listened to some audio tapes of Gururaj teaching.

I'm not a cult person or guru person. I'm a pragmatic, intuitive person. I follow my internal compass, and it has never steered me wrong. I really didn't care if he called himself "peanut butter and jelly." It didn't make any difference what his tag line was. Instinctively, I recognized that he had the gift of shining light on the path that I was walking. It was not the lecture or his techniques, but the tone of voice—the simple and honest way he spoke—that struck a chord and said to me, "This is something we should try."

As it turned out, the only teacher in the United States trained to teach the personalized meditation techniques, suited to us individually and selected for us by Gururaj himself in South Africa, happened to live in Las Vegas.

What are the odds?

I flew the entire family—my mother, Laura, our two little girls, and me—back to Las Vegas (back home in a way) so that Laura and I could learn the personalized meditation practices.

The only way I evaluate something is by the effect it has in my life. In the case of doing Gururaj's meditation practices regularly, I experienced a quantum shift in the way I thought, felt, and perceived others and the world around me. That hole in the black wall that I had envisioned in the beginning days of TM, that had grown larger as I practiced meditation over the years, suddenly—and quickly—got a whole lot bigger. I wasn't walled off anymore from the more essential part of who I was. I felt a sense of "at-home-ness," the ability to be in complete silence where there's nothing going on, except that I was awake (not asleep) inside. When nothing was going on, there was complete peace—no conflicting energies.

I experienced a level of deep relaxation and peace of mind and heart that I had not experienced before. I found that my inner self (the silent but ever-creative observer) began to unfold more and more—so much so that when I went to work, I was more able to deal with the stress of the job, and I was much more creative.

Before going any further in describing my encounter with Gururaj, I want to present who he was and where he came from. The following brief biography was adapted from the American Meditation Society website.

Biography of a Master

Gururaj Ananda Yogi was born in the province of Gujarat, India, on December 12, 1932, to a well-to-do business and farming family. As a child he displayed a remarkably advanced spiritual awareness. Already by the age of three, his questions consistently concerned the meaning and purpose of life and the possibility of truly knowing or experiencing God.

At the age of four-and-a-half, he ran away from home to seek a personal experience of communion with the Divine. He wandered from village to village for nearly six months, living off the food offerings left at temples for the gods. His frantic parents finally found him ragged and barefoot wandering through a village street. When questioned, he explained that he went to as many temples as possible, but the "gods were lifeless and would not speak to me."

Throughout the rest of his childhood and into his early teen years he lived the normal life of a boy in his culture. The exception to this was his intense desire to directly experience the reality of God. He was taught various philosophies by gurus he encountered, and at the age of eight was given a spiritual practice by a monk who wandered from village to village throughout the Indian countryside. Then, driven by the fire that raged within him, he again left home at the age of thirteen or fourteen to continue his search for the peace, integration, and wholeness that is inherent in the realization of the true Self.

In his early twenties, having completed his studies in English, commerce, and accountancy, he immigrated to South Africa where he had lived with his father for three years as a child, thereby establishing rights of residency. There he entered into a business career. Having attained the self-realized state at a very young age, he had constant access to the immense inner resource of the super-conscious mind. Possessing indefatigable energy and a highly refined intuition, he was extremely successful as a businessman and became the director of a number of companies. He married and, with great love and devotion, he and his wife raised three sons. Throughout those years, he also was very active in the Indian community.

About 1974, his worldly vocation came to an end, and he began his time as a spiritual master. In 1975, Gururaj founded the International Foundation for Spiritual Unfoldment. He had begun teaching in South Africa, but then extended his teaching into England, America, Canada, Spain, Denmark, Belgium, Ireland, Israel, Germany, and Cyprus.

Universal Truths

From my personal experience, the teachings of Gururaj Ananda Yogi were simple, understandable, and accessible to anyone, regardless of their background. He spoke to universal truths that are engrained in the heart of every human being. Some part of each person resonates with the truth that his words carry and point to.

Down through the ages, all great masters exhibited the truth that they experienced, whether they started religions that people followed, or whether they were simply humble people. Gururaj was like that.

He walked his talk. The teachings that he gave, he lived. His life was the direct expression of his teachings. He lived his life with integrity and fearlessly, regardless of what anyone thought of the way he should behave or how he should appear in his role as a guru or teacher. He taught the truth as he perceived it, as he lived it, not what other people expected. If you look beyond the words and observe how he interacted, how he lived, he put on no airs. He did not make himself special in any way. The love he gave so unhesitatingly never failed to touch the hearts of all those around him, no matter their personal lives, their troubles and joys. He touched everyone around him in a profound way, and their lives were changed forever.

Though it may take the seed some time to blossom, when it is in full bloom, not only is the flower beautiful but it enhances the beauty of the whole garden. When we make ourselves more beautiful with love, compassion, and understanding, we enhance the beauty of our society and our entire world. Each of us affects not only our immediate surroundings, but like a ripple in a pond, what we do affects all of creation. This is how I understood Gururaj's teachings.

I hope that I can convey in some small measure a sense of the fundamental truths he taught, not just by words, but also by the example of his life. In this book, I do my best to bring out some of his key teachings in the context of my own life. He was a teacher for the ordinary person in Western culture; he lived that life himself.

The Guru's Rest Stop at Our Illinois Home

On a trip to America from his home in South Africa in 1977, Gururaj stayed at our house in Stelle for a couple of days to rest up before going on to teach a course in Santa Barbara, California. The meeting was set up through his traveling companions who knew that we lived on the way.

It was a Saturday afternoon when he knocked on our door. I opened it and this little brown guy, dapper in a suit and tie, stood smoking a cigarette. I had visions of what an enlightened person might look like, but this enlightened dude looked as normal as I was! (He was about forty-five years old. I was thirty-one.) What's more, as a singer, I was impressed with his gorgeous baritone voice with a slight British accent.

I was a little awed, though not worshipful. Here was somebody who had walked the walk and professed to understand the essence of what human life was about and he was visiting in my house!

I said to myself, "Aha, I have an opportunity here."

Gururaj's travelling companions and Laura and the girls were elsewhere in the house. Gururaj and I were sitting in the living room, just the two of us. We both had a drink of Johnnie Walker scotch on the rocks. I decided to ask *the* question. No loopholes. Precise. Exact in wording that would leave no doubt about exactly what I was asking—a synthesis of all the questions I had asked in my entire life (if you think that is easy, try it sometime).

"What is it that I must do in this life to achieve the highest state of consciousness that is possible within a human body?"

I thought it was a pretty good question. I expected some long and profound dissertation.

He took a puff on his cigarette, looked at me, and said two words.

"Seek balance." That was it!

End of the discussion. He didn't say another word in answer.

CHAPTER EIGHT

My Path for the Rest of My Life

Drop by drop is the water pot filled. Likewise, the wise man, gathering it little by little, fills himself with good. — One of Buddha's teachings from the classic *Dhammapada*

S eek balance, he said. That is exactly what he said and nothing else! Very direct, simple, to the point. It was, in retrospect, the only thing he could have said to me. Two words. My teaching. My path for the rest of my entire life was a constant expression of those two words.

Gradually I would fully understand the essence of what Gururaj was teaching me, though I was slow to grasp it during my first encounter with him. He wanted me to find that motionless center point that was neither here nor there, nor high nor low—the ultimate balance point between all opposites where there is silence but infinite potential manifesting as everything and anything spontaneously—and that was within ME! That was the "home" I had been longing for my entire life. He knew those two words—Seek Balance—would in time make more and more sense to me on my path of awakening.

His words, like seeds sown in my heart, had the potential to sprout and grow from a seedling into a sapling, into a giant oak of understanding.

Think about it. The entire universe is working on this balancing of energies and forces. When all energies are focused on that single balance point, they are perfectly still. What's going on in that stillness? There's nothing going on, only pure awareness without content, undifferentiated (without form), clear; diamond-hard reality not cluttered and covered over by the movements of manifested phenomena. This is the essential nature of all human kind, of all creation. It is within us—it is home!

A singular seamless reality of pure awareness manifesting as all name and form is abstract in the extreme, but I will do my best to give a simple explanation in the form of a metaphor. It's like a three-dimensional hologram. If you break the holographic picture into a thousand shards and then look at one piece, the entire picture will be in that one piece, but seen from the angle of view of that one shard. So it is with all of us. We have the imprint of all creation within us. The "One" expresses itself as the many, and the many is the expression of the "One" eternal principle of pure awareness, whose innate potential appears spontaneously as all manifest creation.

First Impressions

I'm not a philosopher, a scholar, or a theologian. But I know when someone is speaking the truth at a more fundamental, deeper level than what is being said on the surface. Something within me knows when the underlying truth is within what is being said, or when that underlying truth is missing. Call it my internal Truth barometer or bullshit-o-meter. It's never played me false. I confirmed for myself at our first face-to-face meeting that Gururaj was, in fact, the real deal—at least for me. I do not mean to say that he was the right teacher for everyone, but I can say with certainty he was the right teacher for me.

When Gururaj told me to seek balance, the absolute truth of that one statement was the only key that fit the lock of my heart. It is difficult to put into words, but it was an internal sense of finding the truth I had been searching for since starting my journey reading philosophy books in Vietnam. For me, the clarity and precision within those two words contained all I needed to reach my (our) ultimate home, and could only come from a realized master.

Laura and I had just kind of hit it off really well with Gururaj immediately. We accompanied him to the course at the University of California in Santa Barbara. It was to be a five-day course, and his supporters had done some great publicity to register more than a hundred people.

On the way to Santa Barbara, Gururaj and I sat together on the plane from Chicago to San Francisco.

Half the time he held my hand. I had no real idea why.

He had closed his eyes. So I closed mine, though I peeked out every once in a while. It was like being somewhere else, not in that body on that airplane, but being in a very dark space. I couldn't describe it as a place in space or time. I couldn't put my finger on it, but I didn't particularly care to at that point. It was what it was, and I experienced a great and overwhelming peace. That was good enough for me.

After a while, he let go of my hand. He looked at me with a quirky little grin on his face.

"How was the ride?" he said.

"Interesting," I said. What else was I going to say? There I was, analytical, empirical, no-nonsense. Though I had deep philosophical interests, I wasn't your flaky flower child or groupie. I was definitely not the type of person who expounded at length about some mystical experience. I just couldn't really attach any significance to it. I simply accepted the experience and let it go.

Sujay Is Born

It was at the course at UC Santa Barbara, our first one, that Gururaj gave me my spiritual name. He had been calling me "Bob" for the few days we had known him, almost like he had a bad taste in his mouth. It was unusual how he said it. It felt like a stone hitting the floor. I thought it wasn't a bad name—it was short, easy to remember, and fairly common.

I remember sitting on the registrar's counter swinging my feet back and forth, by myself and not doing anything. All of a sudden, Gururaj opened the door to the room where he was resting between talks, and waved to me.

"Come here."

I jumped off the counter and went into the room with him.

"Stand here," he said.

He had in his arms the Namaste picture of himself, flowers, and a candle. The word Namaste means, "I bow to the divine within you." In the photo, he had his hands held palm-to-palm at the level of his heart (picture the praying hands position as in the Christian tradition). The word and the gesture honor the divine spark within each of us.

He did a ceremony, which in Sanskrit is called a Puja, or prayer. This is an Eastern tradition. I had respect for that, but I didn't have a weighty feeling about it one way or the other. It was a prayer traditionally used when people were initiated into meditation practices. Laura and I had heard it before. It was beautiful delivered in person in his resonant voice.

Then he told me to sit down in a chair. He put his hands on my head from behind and repeated three times, "I confer upon you the name 'Sujay.' "

When I got up, he told me what my new name meant— Su (goodness) and Jay (victor, or bringer). Translated: bringer of goodness, or he who has victory through goodness. I also found out that a spiritual name doesn't say what you are but, rather, what you have the capability to be. You use the name as a reminder of what you need to get more in touch with in yourself. Being mindful and conscious of this responsibility, being diligent and working, you slowly grow into the essence of the meaning of the name. It is really an admonition, a call to duty, or even a burden, because it gives you no choice. You can't plead ignorance.

Getting a new name is like coming of age. You have a certain level of understanding and responsibilities that go with them. I had experienced Gururaj's initiation, but other traditions have similar ceremonies—in the Catholic tradition it would be like the sacrament of confirmation, a time to shoulder responsibility as Jesus bids you to pick up your cross and walk with him.

People at the course were very eager to get a spiritual name, but as a virtual newcomer, it meant almost nothing to me at the time.

During the evening talk, or Satsang, which means "in the presence of truth," Gururaj said, "I would like you all to meet Sujay. Bob no longer is. Sujay has been born."

I was a little embarrassed, naturally. Everyone looked at me a little enviously, and I still didn't know what the hell was going on or what it meant, though "Sujay" had a nice ring.

The word goodness has elements of compassion in it, kindness, selflessness, the ability to put others before oneself or one's own interests. It has a lot of cousins and uncles and aunts. As the meaning of my new name sank deeper into my understanding, it became a sacred obligation to be better than I am.

So, that's how I got my alternate name, Sujay. Most of my AMS friends call me Suj, for short. But in the work world, and to my friends beyond the circle of meditators in the American Meditation Society, I'm still Bob.

About a year after the Santa Barbara course, in the context of another course, Laura got her spiritual name. Gururaj related that she came to him in a dream and said, "Bapuji (father), don't you know who I am?" And he said, "Of course, I know who you are, Vidya." Her name means divine knowledge.

CHAPTER NINE

Craziness and Wisdom Converge

Guru, God and Self are One. — from the spiritual teachings of the great mystic of India, Ramana Marharshi (1879-1950)

W e didn't make a big announcement about it, but Laura and I stopped teaching TM as soon as we began using Gururaj's practices. We didn't drop our students, didn't abandon them, but we didn't take on new TM students. After about six months, we made the transition to teaching Gururaj's techniques.

We went to numerous courses after the first one in Santa Barbara. And Gururaj would live with us in our home for a month or two at a time in between courses he held in the United States. I got to know him very well.

Having a guru in the house is not what most people would think. We'd sit around and tell jokes, have a scotch—or two—and smoke a cigarette now and then. Gururaj loved my charcoal-grilled barbecued chicken—it was one of his favorite meals. But then, in the middle of eating dinner and talking about mundane things, he would interweave just a sentence or two of poetic, beautiful wisdom that would go through the mind and hit the heart immediately. Like a gong being struck. Like, "Wake up!"

Early on, Vidya began travelling with Gururaj all over the United States, all over the world sometimes, as his administrative assistant. She helped him with all courses held by the American Meditation

Society, which he founded. At the same time, I was rising in my career at Armour, then Revlon. I was flying all over the country on special projects. I was part of a mergers-and-acquisitions team analyzing the information technology side of the businesses to see how to integrate them into the Revlon infrastructure.

My mother, Irene, took care of our little girls when both Vidya and I had to be away.

Balancing our lives during those years was not easy by any stretch of the imagination. We had our share of friction. Our connection to family was profound. Our connection to Gururaj was equally compelling. Holding everything together was our strong belief that everything we were attempting was essential both to ourselves and to many, many others.

FAMILY
In the back, Bob and daughters, Colleen and Crystal.
In the front, his wife, Vidya, on the left, and his mother, Irene.

To distill Gururaj's teachings and practices and capture the essence of his wisdom in a few chapters of a book is difficult. He delivered hundreds of satsangs on his journey and delivered individual techniques that deepened meditation practice for countless individuals. Some of his teachings began to be preserved in books and some of his satsangs on DVD and CD were made available through the hard work of American Meditation Society members.

The AMS website gives this description of Gururaj's work: With inexhaustible energy, he traveled from country to country, holding meditation retreats of about a week at a time. Often teaching far into the night, he shared the wisdom he had gained from his own experience on the spiritual path. He considered himself a universalist and taught the essence of the teachings that underlie all the world's major religions. In the time-honored methods of the oral tradition, he would sit with his chelas, or students, and they would ask questions and he would answer for an hour or so. He never prepared a talk. He spoke directly from the heart, the core of the human personality and taught the welling up of joy that comes from meditations and spiritual practices that make humans receptive to the flow of grace.

Unconditional Love

During the first couple of years of our relationship, Gururaj was gentle with me. At courses, I would sit with him before the morning talk, help get his tea, then I'd walk with him to the meeting hall.

He was very loving and caring. One of the really nice things I remember was a ritual we had when we travelled together. Every day I would sit and talk with him while he shaved. He used a razor and foam.

In that delightful British accent he said, "Now Sujay, this is how you shave. You go down this way and up this way." Then, motioning to his cheek, he would say, "Feel that? See how smooth it is?" Even today I smile every morning when I shave, remembering those times.

Before evening satsangs, we'd often sit in his room and agonize over a book of 10,000 jokes. He'd speak very openly, and said, "The Divine Force flows through me so strongly that I never think before I speak. I just sit and cross my legs and whatever personality I have is gone." That power simply spoke to that which was needful within the people who were there, an inner knowing beyond the rational mind. He had a way of just knowing, and speaking from that point of knowingness, so that he would always touch the heart of the issue that was under discussion. It was as if he were reading our minds. Many times he would say what I was thinking word for word.

The first time we looked at jokes together, he said to me, "I have a hard time lightening things up. People can only stand so much of this really deep stuff and then their brains get fried. So, I need your help finding some jokes." We'd pore over the stupid book of inane jokes and pick some out. He would write down the punch line on a little slip of paper and put it at his side when he was delivering the talk. He'd look down at a couple of key words to recall the joke, but invariably he would screw up the telling.

I'd be falling off my chair laughing so hard. He would take a simple joke and screw it up so bad. But he would tell it in such an engaging way and laugh all the while because he knew he was screwing it up. Just that lightness would lift up the mood! Those precious moments I remember. After the talk, we'd have our usual couple of Johnnie Walker scotches and a cigarette.

"He'd say, How was it Suj? How did it sound?"

I'd say, "Fine, Bapuji, just fine." And it was! Bapuji was my spiritual father.

My biological father provided the genetic material and an intellectual push in my teens. Gururaj was the one who really shaped and molded whatever character, goodness, and spiritual understanding was in me and enhanced them, though I didn't work with him until I was in my early thirties. We had a very special and loving relationship. But he never told me what to do.

He didn't say stop eating meat. Or become a vegetarian.

He didn't say don't have sex.

He didn't say stop smoking.

Or stop drinking.

What he did say, however, most vehemently, was, "Be yourself. Never let anyone tell you how to live your life. Have courage to live from your own convictions." He was adamant.

That made sense to me. If all of a sudden he had tried to manipulate my life, then I would have backed away. Instead, he accepted me and

96

loved me for all my warts and shortcomings. Complete unconditional love was new for me. I had only experienced that with my mother, and she had to love me unconditionally because it came with her job description.

Integrity and Courage

His unconditional love for me certainly was not based on my being incredibly lovable. I was a scruffy nerf herder! I was a businessman rough around the edges. But I was a good Marine. And many of Gururaj's teachings aligned with values I'd learned in the Corps. In those values, Gururaj and I seemed to have a natural affinity.

Gururaj insisted upon integrity and courage in the pursuit of my questions: Why am I here and what is the universe about? And he reinforced my instinct to find my own answers—I couldn't read a book, even the *Bible*, and take it as absolute truth. I had to experience something firsthand for myself and only then could it become real for me, become part of me. That's how I'm built.

As a Marine, I had honed my ability to rely on my instincts (required in combat), and I had the courage to stand upon the rock of my own convictions. Win, lose, or draw. That held me in good stead as I met the spiritual challenges Gururaj presented to me. He guided me to live up to my potential, to find the reason that this body and personality came into existence. He would say, "Nobody comes here by accident."

The Worshipful Guru Thing

Though he loved me unconditionally, that's not to say that Gururaj put up with my crap or anybody else's. In the early days, some of his devotees tried to wall him off and perpetuate the mystique of putting the guru on a pedestal. I wasn't having any part of that. Neither was he, by the way. When people tried to put him on a pedestal, he went out of his way to absolutely destroy the idea of some graven image or golden calf they had in their minds of what a guru was supposed to be like.

He would take it for a while, but then he would do something so outrageous that would endear him to the "maverick" in me (my call sign, or nickname, when I was flying and also a trait identified by a psychologist in my personality evaluation).

He'd get up and say, "Fuck all of you," or "You don't know what the fuck you are doing!"

Some would say, "Oh my God! He said fuck! He can't be holy. He said a bad word!"

Now, spiritual teachers sometimes seem crazy as coots, but you can't tell a self-realized (enlightened) man only by his outward actions. Motivation and outcome define the true teacher, and virtually all the time we have no knowledge of "real" motivation behind the Master's actions. We get these images or concepts of what a holy person or a realized person is, a good person is, and if they don't fit our narrow definitions, or our little mold, we throw them on the garbage heap. Then we go away and look for the next showman to entertain us by our standards. Gururaj wasn't about that. He was holding up a mirror for people to see themselves. Typically very few people have the courage to look at themselves honestly, admitting their faults and shortcomings to themselves. He so much wanted each person to find their own inner guru (their own inner teacher, their true self). He was not going to be another crutch to lean on. He was compassionate, but he would not put up with any guru worship

"The only thing you should worship is within you," he would say. "Don't look at me. Listen to my words. Try them out. If they work, then fine; if they don't, then let them go."

Master of Parody

Somehow amid all the craziness and all the beautiful wisdom, Vidya and I, along with a few others, stuck with him. We could have made no other choice. We stayed because we saw beyond his outrageous facade. For me, he was the only game in town that I could say was a man with no other agenda than to get people, including me, to look at themselves and see the illusion that they had perpetuated and identified as truth.

He was brilliant at parody.

He'd walk through an airport with us and say with pretended arrogance for all to hear, "I'm the vice president of dah, dah, dah…." I could have crawled under a sheet of toilet paper with headroom to spare. I would hide in a corner while Vidya and one or two other brave souls would stay next to him.

I only see things clearly in retrospect. He knew every button I had and exactly which ones to push. I had an overblown sense of self-importance and propriety, of doing things a certain way because I was told this was the way you are supposed to act or behave as "a successful business executive." I put myself in a little imaginary identity box. I was, after all, an executive who was in demand throughout a large corporation. I'd fallen in love with my own false image, my own golden calf. I made the terrible mistake of believing my own fantasy built by the ego.

Remember the old saying, "Pride cometh before the fall"? Well, I was setting myself up for a doozy.

Through parody, Gururaj was telling me, "This is the way you are behaving, not because it's you inside, but because society has told you how to behave." He was trying desperately to warn me of what I was doing, and that my behavior basically was building up false ideas of self—false, graven images of my own false god: the EGO!

Staring Down the Tiger

The man was absolutely fearless. He told me a story once about going through the jungle on the way to his guru's house. A tiger crossed the path in front of him and looked at him as if, "Here's the noonday meal." An animal senses fear, so Gururaj said, "Come, if this body can feed you, go at it. Have fun."

He stood there staring down the tiger. The tiger looked at him and then walked away.

Some would say, "Maybe the tiger just wasn't hungry." Be that as it may, I had never known anybody else who was completely fearless. I'd known brave men in combat in Vietnam. But that's not the same as being completely fearless.

Gururaj was.

By normal human standards of behavior, Gururaj might be classified as an absolute madman. He was highly unpredictable, capable of putting on an Academy Award-level act whenever he thought it necessary. He was a master at playing the drunken guru, for example. One evening at my house he and I put away almost a bottle and a half of Johnnie Walker scotch in my bar downstairs. Both he and I had not the faintest trace of fuzziness of the brain or slurred speech, and we were both sober as judges. Normally three scotches would have had me on my ass. This time I might as well have been drinking tap water—what a waste of good scotch! There was some subtle energy within and around him that when a particular situation required, he could completely negate the effects of the alcohol on the human body. OK, I know it sounds crazy, but I have no other explanation. Remember, I was there. I did it.

On the other hand, I had also seen him act the stumbling, drunken fool after one shot when he was in a gathering of people who tended toward "the worshipful guru thing."

The lesson I took away was: Don't judge a book by its cover or judge by arbitrary standards of behavior, and don't presume to know how a person should look or act based on your own preconceived notions and beliefs. This was not just for the guru in this case, but anybody. We do terrible injustice to others by making snap judgments based on little or no information. How small-minded, small-hearted, and even cruel we can be.

I learned to refer to Gururaj as a teacher or guide, somebody who shines the light on the path. He would say, "I can shine the light on the path, but the steps must be yours. It's your journey. I took the same journey. It is your divine right to find your True Self." He taught me to shed all my preconceived notions of right and wrong and to find out for myself what's true—good or bad—for *me*, not for everyone else. He told me to take one step at a time and not to worry about some fictional or imagined end state of enlightenment or utopia. Pay attention to NOW; all the rest takes care of itself, as it has done since the first instant of creation.

He reinforced lessons I had learned throughout my life, especially in the Marine Corps—to be responsible for myself, not to blame anyone or anything else for my difficult times and problems, and to be courageous.

And he taught me how to find what connects me with all of creation and say with absolute certainty that "I and my Father are one."

We can all say that, for none of us is different in our essential nature from each other or anything else in creation.

A lot of guru guys out there do tricks and thrive on ritual guru worship. Gururaj was the absolute antithesis of that. He didn't put on any airs. He behaved as if to say: Don't worship me. Look within yourself. That is the guru you should worship. If you put me on a pedestal, I'll do all kinds of crazy things that will drive you stark-raving mad. One of two things will happen—your unconditional love will be strong enough so that you'll stay with me and you will understand, or you will go away.

He had a way of separating the wheat from the chaff, the diamonds from the coal. But, he would always take anyone back, as if they had never left. Again, unconditional love in action.

**Bob sings in the background while in the foreground
Gururaj prays that his voice would improve!**

CHAPTER TEN

Sujay Gets His Ass Kicked

Engage people with what they expect; it is what they are able to discern and confirms their projections. It settles them into predictable patterns of response, occupying their minds while you wait for the extraordinary moment—that which they cannot anticipate. — from the book *The Art of War* (610 B.C.), *by Sun Tzu, Chinese warrior-philosopher*

I don't know if Gururaj had ever read *The Art of War* by Sun Tzu, though I suspect he had in this life or a previous one. It's the 2,000-year-old Taoist-inspired volume about outfoxing the enemy and winning battles, but it explains so many of Gururaj's teaching behaviors. He was an expert spiritual warrior.

Generally, walking the spiritual path alongside Gururaj was amazing because of his wonderful insights and exceptional articulation of spiritual truths, his patience, and his unconditional love. And for the first couple of years, as I've described, things were very mellow. But as soon as I trusted fully that I was loved, it was time for me to grow up.

Let it be known that I am particularly stubborn and bull-headed. Those who know me are saying with mock surprise right now, "Oh, really?" I've never learned things the easy way. Mother always said, "You'll learn it through your head or you'll learn it through your butt." I'm a butt-learner. A whack every now and again gets my attention.

So Gururaj was not easy on me when I'd get uppity or make a smartass remark. One night, I remember, I was really ticked off at him because he had said something I didn't like to someone I liked. I was listening from my own very small perspective. He was speaking from the point of view of spontaneously responding to the need of the moment. People generally communicate in one of two ways: They speak from their old tapes, conditioning, and memory, or they speak from complete innocence, from an intuitive knowing about the point of view and needs of another individual at that moment in time.

That I couldn't understand his motives was irrelevant. He was doing his job as he saw fit. On this particular day, I gave him a ration of crap and then I escaped into another room where I sat down with my feet up on a chair.

He came into the room walking with a cane—his health was deteriorating because he pushed himself so hard. He was a diabetic and had a heart condition. I'll never forget it. He came into the room and Vidya came in with him. He raised his cane over his head and came down full force on my shin, not once but twice. And I had shorts on!

Vidya went goofy.

"What are you doing? You're hitting him! You'll break his leg," she cried frantically.

I didn't crack a smile or make a grimace. Nothing! I was hit but it didn't hurt.

Bapuji said to me in a perfectly normal voice, "Suj, what's wrong with her?"

I shrugged and said, "I don't know."

A stout walking cane can bust a shin or at least break the skin and leave a goose egg big enough to hang your hat on. Strangely enough, there was not a bruise on my leg where he whacked me. And he was a strong man, despite his illnesses! There was not even a red mark or welt. Don't ask me about some of these things, because I have no way of explaining them in words that would make any sense to anyone who wasn't there.

Sujay got his ass kicked many times thereafter. Big time. Hugely. Frequently. But always with love and always with the intent that I not get stuck in my personal ego, in arrogance, or in a make-believe world. Instinctively I knew that. Though I couldn't understand intellectually what Gururaj did sometimes, I had unconditional faith and trust that whatever he did was for my betterment.

I cannot speak for how others would or should have reacted to this event if they had been in my shoes, but for me it was like during those moments, time was suspended. In a heartbeat there was an altered reality, looking basically the same to most of the senses, but 20 degrees out of phase. Hence, no pain, no welt, no broken bones or skin. I experienced this as clearly as the heat of the sun on a cloudless summer day. Another lesson I learned from this event was that things are not always what they appear to be. The surface action may have nothing to do with what is really happening. Many years passed before I knew this, not with the mind but with my intuitive and emotional center—the heart.

Fingernail or Fork to the Forehead

In Eastern spiritual tradition, there is something called the eye of wisdom, or the third eye, right in the center of the forehead. If one is familiar with the chakras, it is the spot where the ajna chakra is located and is associated with intuition, visualization, and creativity.

One evening after dinner, Gururaj told me to sit still, that he was going to give me a practice that Ramakrishna gave to Vivekananda to speed him to self-realization. Ramakrishna was a very famous sage of

106

the latter half of the nineteenth century, and Vivekananda was his chief disciple who traveled around the world spreading the word of self-realization and freedom from suffering.

Well, as I sat there at our kitchen table, Gururaj dug the fingernail of his thumb into my forehead between my eyes.

"Do you feel that pain?" he said.

I said, "Do I look unconscious? Of course I feel the pain."

"Now close your eyes and allow your attention to be where that pain is." He explained that wherever your awareness is, there goes energy.

A meditation technique called Tratak operates on the same principle. You look at a candle flame, then allow your gaze to rest gently on the after-image when you close your eyes. It teaches effortless concentration and a gentle focusing of the mind, which allows one to concentrate on things for a long period of time without getting tired.

Periodically over the years, Gururaj would take whatever was at hand and dig it into the center of my forehead. One time it was a fork tine. I would focus on the pain without effort and feel the energy flow to that point. Another time he took a steak knife. It drew blood. I have a scar right in the center of my forehead that I can feel even today, more than twenty-five years later.

He hit the same exact spot every time, as if he had a micrometer. Talk about an accurate shot. He made my accuracy at the pistol range look like a rank amateur. He never hesitated. Boom! Right to the same exact spot every time.

The funny thing was that, over time, I began to notice when I was thinking that images would begin to form in the mind. If I were at work, I wouldn't try to think of a solution. The solution would build itself in visual form in incredible detail. I would start writing it down or talking to people, basically narrating what I was seeing. It was nothing that I as an individual could take credit for. Images coalesced from vaporous thought within the screen of the mind and linked together to form a beautiful mosaic that would be the precise solution to a problem I happened to be working on.

There was something to this mystical business that I couldn't explain from a scientific or empirical point of view, but only with a line from Shakespeare's *Hamlet*: "There are more things in heaven and earth, Horatio, than are dreamt of in your philosophy."

So many lessons. But the "fork to the forehead" technique especially resonates: Keep an open mind. One should wait and see what kind of results happen before casting judgments on the methods.

Is That the Best You've Got?

Another time, our family had moved from our home in Illinois to a new home in Pennsylvania, and Gururaj was staying with us. I was coming out of my bedroom and he was going in to lie down. We met each other in the doorway. He was 5′6″, a little shorter than me, but we were about nose to nose. He stopped and stared at me.

He said, "Sujay, why are you here?"

I'm thinking to myself. "What the hell kind of question is that? I'm here in the doorway, just got off from work a little while ago, and I want to change clothes and relax."

Then I caught on and said aloud, "I'm here to earn a living, provide for my family, be the best person I know how to be, not make waves, try to help people where I can, and that's about it."

As I was speaking, I noticed he was slumping to one side almost like his shoulder hurt. What I didn't know was that he was reaching toward the floor so he could gain momentum for his next move.

With a calm face, not even a twitch, he said, "That's not it."

Then he straightened up, and bringing his left hand up and across he hit the side of my head, so hard that I saw stars. That was the first time I had ever been slugged hard enough to see stars.

I was angry for a second and said, "What the hell is this? Is that the best you've got?"

Then he walked on into the bedroom and lay down. We never talked about it again.

My anger vanished as quickly as it had come. Later on it occurred to me that, as usual, I was asleep to my true purpose in life, and he was trying to wake me up. Seems my mission in life was to be a bit more than raising a family and holding down a good job. At least, I got that much from the smack upside the head. But I'm still trying to figure that one out. Maybe writing this book is part of the answer that I'm living into. Only time will tell.

There were countless experiences like that, where he did things that I never imagined a spiritual master would do. Different folks, friends, and family would react in different ways to my unusual exchanges with Gururaj. For me they were simply events, and I carried no emotional load away from them. The greater teaching was what mattered to me.

To the best of my knowledge, I was the only one he teed off on (whacked the hell out of). Probably for one reason: I was particularly hard-headed and, as I have said, I was a kick-in-the-butt learner.

Trust me. You hang out with Marine Corps drill instructors for thirteen weeks during the 1960s and I guarantee you will become quite accustomed to harsh treatment. Gururaj knew I was especially able to withstand the toughness, see it in the right perspective, and profit from the lessons. This is just a guess, but as good as any.

These events, and so many more to come, validated for me that I had made the right decision to stay with Gururaj and learn all I could.

CHAPTER ELEVEN

Shouldering Sorrows in Cyprus

You never know how strong you are until being strong is the only choice you have. — Unknown

W e were taking a "spiritual holiday" with some of the people who were closest to Gururaj, going to Cyprus for two weeks in March 1987. I had some vacation time saved up from work, and had saved a little money. About twenty of us from the meditation societies in England, Spain, the United States, the United Kingdom, Denmark, Ireland, and Canada stayed in a couple of hotels near Limassol, Cyprus.

A number of people thought it was big vacation time, so they toured the island. I intuited the trip differently as described below. I might add that I was used to extraordinary things happening by this point.

Gururaj did things that were super human. He would teach twenty-four hours a day from sun-up around the clock to sunup again. I'm not sure if he ever slept. He would just teach and teach and teach: the greatest teachings from thousands of years, but not history lessons or religious texts, per se. He taught truths that applied to each person individually and to all of humankind. It was like going to a huge food market and having all the food that's just right for you served up especially for you. I was in awe of his skill.

A couple of interesting things happened for me in Cyprus. First, I got the third-eye routine again. We were in his room lying down. This time it was very different. He gently touched the center of my forehead with his middle finger. It was like somebody had ignited a blow torch on the site. Whatever was going on, that was the culmination of the third-eye technique for me. Something shattered, or exploded, in a brilliant flash of light. God forbid that anyone else would have touched my forehead thereafter—I would have gone unconscious from the pain. It was ten years before I could even touch it. I would wash my face, but I did it really quick because I would wince every time my hand went over the center of my forehead. Even today, when I put my fingers over my forehead, I still feel that throbbing.

It was the damnedest thing.

Goofball Groaning on Stage

No matter how accustomed I became to extraordinary happenings, I still cringed when Gururaj behaved outrageously in public. One evening in Cyprus we all decided to go out to dinner together. On this occasion, he surprised us with an unusually wild and crazy performance. If I had known beforehand what he would to do this time, I would have run as far and as fast as I could in the other

direction. But there I was, fat, dumb, and happy. We picked a restaurant where we could listen to some Greek Cypriot entertainers.

The first thing Gururaj did was to have a couple of our young ladies, one a dear friend of mine, Usha, go around the restaurant talking to people about meditation. I thought that was pretty weird, but I let it go. The first act came up, and we had a drink or two and appetizers. Then what did he do? He got up, climbed onto the stage, grabbed the microphone, and started crooning. More like groaning. He had a lovely singing voice, by the way, but this was a performance of the "crazy guru" kind.

With my predisposed sense of propriety (my Achilles heel was going to take an arrow), I thought, "Ah, damn, here we go. Here are all these people in the restaurant who are trying to eat their dinner. And this goofball is on stage groaning at them in the microphone."

He put the mic down and came over to me and said, "Suj, that's pretty good, huh?"

Out of the corner of my eye, I could see the look of distress on the owner's face.

I said, "Bapuji, please don't do that. Look at all these people—you are screwing up their evening. The next act is going to come onstage. Please sit down."

Gururaj ignored me and went back on stage, back to groaning in God knows what language. While he was up there this time, the owner came over to me.

"Sir, obviously you know this gentleman."

"Yes, I do."

"Can you please have him come sit down so the next act can come up? He's disturbing all the other patrons."

Gururaj came off stage, and asked me again, "Suj, wasn't that good?" I said, "Bapuji, look, the owner asked me if you would please not do that. I'm asking you now, please sit down and let's have a drink and dinner."

"No, they love me," he said, "I'm going back up there."

I said, "We're going to do this the easy way or the hard way. You are not going back."

He started toward the stage. I grabbed him around the chest with my arms. I was strong. I was a physical fitness trainer at that time. I lifted weights for two hours a day, three days a week. But this guy almost overpowered me flailing his arms. I could not believe how strong he was. I maintained my hold.

I begged him, "Please. Please don't do this." Then, "OK. It looks like the hard way."

I threw him over my shoulders in a fireman's carry. I walked out of the restaurant with him to the applause of all of the patrons. The meditators who were with us surely thought, "Oh my god, he's manhandling the guru! He's gonna get fried."

I got him outside and reality did a flip-flop. I no longer had a man on my shoulders. I could feel the weight of the sorrows of the entire planet on my shoulders. I honestly felt like I was being crushed, not from his weight because he wasn't that heavy. I didn't know where this was coming from and had no way of rationalizing it. All I knew was that the mental anguish and sorrow were unbearable.

I could feel the suffering of all humanity pressing down on me. I put him down. Damn, he was mad as a wet mouse!

"Sujay, you son of a bitch."

I was almost unconscious. I could barely stand up. Whatever that weight was, the unbearable sorrow, when I put him down it vanished immediately. But it drained the last ounce of energy from my body. I was staggering, but not from alcohol consumption. A meditator from England and his wife had followed us out of the restaurant. They saw that I was terribly weakened, so he got under one arm, his wife under the other. They practically carried me back to their hotel room, across the street from where Gururaj was staying.

I was in a daze. I didn't know what had happened. I immediately had a double scotch to reorient to this reality. I sat completely drained, shredded internally, and shaking. About forty minutes later, I heard a knock on the door. It was Usha, my friend from England whom Gururaj had instructed to tell people about meditation at the restaurant. She saw me on the couch and said, "Gururaj has the entire course all over the island looking for you. Where have you been?"

I thought, "Oh crap, he's going to turn me into a cinder. I'm so totally screwed."

I figured he was just going to rake me over the coals and God knows what else, given the kind of power I felt when he was on my shoulders. I was getting ready to basically leave this body.

I said to myself, "OK, suck it up, Marine. It's time to face the music."

I got up and walked across the courtyard like a man going to his hanging or

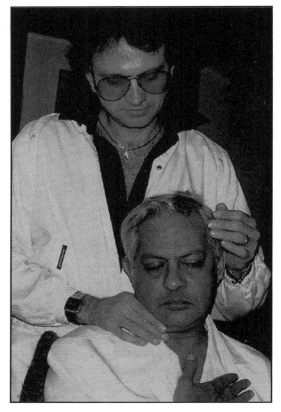

execution. I took the stairs up to his room. People I knew were watching me like, "I wouldn't be him for all the money in the world."

Gururaj was lying on the bed. He looked at me like nothing ever happened.

"Sujay, I've been so worried about you. Come here my darling. I couldn't find you."

He hugged me and held me close. It was gone, the pain and weakness disappeared instantly. With all the other people standing around in his room, I just put my head on his chest and went to sleep. I was home and it was the most at peace and happiest I'd ever been in my life. What a bizarre set of circumstances.

Who woulda thunk? This stuff didn't happen to me—a working stiff, a combat Marine, a mud slogger. What did I know about all this weird spiritual stuff? But I could not deny the experience or what I felt. You cannot run away from your own experience when it is as intense as that. It was more real to me than a chair or table.

My Christian Roots Deepen and Widen

I learned so much from my experiences with Gururaj. And my Catholic faith never diminished. Instead, it deepened and widened. Gururaj used to talk endlessly about Jesus like they were good buddies. He really "got" Jesus of Nazareth. The more he talked about Him, the more I thought, "Wow, so that's what Jesus was talking about." My knowledge of Christ was deepened by someone who by birth was a Hindu, though he didn't think any more of the Hindu gods than he did of any others.

I began to "get" for myself—on deeper and deeper levels—who and what Jesus Christ was and what He tried to do. He wasn't making a big deal out of himself. He was showing, by living example, that which we also can be and do. He was the ultimate example of integrity, courage, unconditional selflessness, and utter commitment.. There was a man with whom I would storm the gates of hell!

Such great compassion, great unconditional love, and wisdom—traits to model yourself after! How He cared for people—tax collectors, prostitutes, untouchables, lepers! What better example do we have of unconditional love? Not to be motivated by fear of going to hell—that's not courage, but cowardice! Instead, to be moved by love and armored by the courage of our convictions.

"Hell is bullshit. Refuse to live a life out of fear. Live your life from love with courage," Gururaj would say.

Now, love—that I could do. Compassion I could do. Living out of conviction, integrity, and courage...I could also do that. As far as I was concerned, practicing these Christian traits not only strengthened my faith but, more importantly, brought me a sense of joy and personal fulfillment.

Jesus of Nazareth was a revolutionary in his own time. All the Jews and the Sanhedrin and Pharisees were preaching about how to control people through fear and how to get more money out of people's pockets and into theirs. And what was Jesus doing? He was penniless, preaching, "Love ye one another!" If a man strikes you on the cheek, turn to him the other. He spoke in parables of living truth. I don't claim to be able to do that, but I surely admire a man who can.

All other religions have the same fundamental roots if you take time to dig deep enough. If you read the Bhagavad Gita, for example, the central chapters are an epic Hindu poem called the Mahabharata in which Krishna (God incarnate) and Arjuna (a warrior prince) are on a great battlefield. Arjuna was one of the greatest warriors of his time and ready for battle, but Krishna reminded Arjuna that the army he was about to fight included his uncles, brothers, and cousins. By doing so, he transformed Arjuna's lust for battle into love and compassion for his relatives. Only then, when Arjuna's mind was quiet, suspended between these two opposing thoughts, did Krishna unfold the eternal truths of divine wisdom to Arjuna there on the battlefield.

The point, in my experience, is that all religions have love, compassion, and kindness at their core. Through the ages, so many humans have misunderstood and distorted the teachings of great souls. This is at least one reason our societies are in the damned mess we are in today, with brother against brother, nation against nation!

I have found for myself that it is absolutely beautiful how the One Truth expresses itself in so many different forms that we call religions.

118

Gururaj would say, "If you want to be a Christian, be a better Christian. If you are a Buddhist, be a better Buddhist. If you are a Hindu, be a better Hindu. Understand the foundational truths of your beliefs and live them from love and compassion, not out of fear." In fact, the registered emblem of the American Meditation Society represents an acknowledgment of the universal spiritual truth of all religion. Symbols of the world's great religions are arranged around a central lamp, which represents the flame of divinity in each person's heart.

Gururaj respected all, but he always said, "Take a look for yourself at the divine truth that is being expressed by all these religions. See what the founders were really saying, look beyond the doctrines, dogmas, and personality cults built up around them for thousands of years. You will find that One Truth of peace and love shines brightly. Then you will begin to see the truth in all religions."

Jesus said, and I paraphrase, "The things I can do, you will do also, and greater things shall you do (John 14:12)." Others tried to make him one-off and unique. He didn't actually say that. It wasn't until 140 years after his death that the gospels were written. And it was Constantine, at the Nicene Council in 325 A.D., who molded them into what we call today's *Bible*, which had fear and control built in, editing out many of the original gospels. Most religions—Christianity, Buddhism, Islam, Hinduism, and others—have elements of distortion and control built into them. That's how you keep organized religions going and keep people in line with the fear of hell or its equivalent.

However, if we go back to the essential teachings, they are simple. "Thou shalt love the Lord thy God with all thy heart, and with all thy soul, and with all thy strength, and with all thy mind; and thy neighbor as thyself" (Luke 10:27). Love is that divine essence within us. What we truly love unconditionally, we become one with, because love unites all manifest creation. This is how Jesus could say, "I and my

119

Father are one (John 10:30)," and with that same intensity of conviction and unconditional love we also can truthfully say the same thing. The last part, love others as you love yourself sounds easy, but when you really try it, you find that it takes hard work, patience, humility, and surrender to that divine force within. We don't just love some abstract something called divinity, but the entire person no matter how he or she appears to our conscious mind. Culture, religion, or social standing should not influence how we feel. Forgive those who do you harm. Always extend a hand where you can to help someone. If you can't, at least leave that person alone to live in peace. These are simple things. Life is not complicated when we live it closer to the truth. When the underpinning (truth) of religion is pushed into the background and further away from its original truth, when all the trappings of society control and dim that truth, when doctrine, dogma, and ritual take over—that's when the trouble starts.

Christianity, as it is so often taught in churches nowadays, encourages people to denigrate themselves. But that which we believe we become. "I'm a sinner," we say. If, instead, we believe we have divinity within us and strive to express that as love in our lives as best we can, then it does not matter if we fall a thousand times. We will have the courage and strength to get up, dust ourselves off, and try again. It is love, not fear, that gives us the courage and strength to do what must be done and what we know in our heart is right.

That's what Gururaj and Jesus taught me.

The Greatest Cathedral in the World

I do my best to live according to the highest truths that are embodied within all religions—as Christ, Buddha, Krishna, and other great incarnations of truth have lived—to help those who can't help themselves, to unconditionally love, not to hate, not to judge, not to speak ill of others. I fall down a lot, but I fall less and less often, and I am able to get up quicker and keep moving. As well as I can, when I screw up, I admit it and try to learn the lesson it has to teach. Regret and guilt are fruitless. They are like hanging stones around your neck, a weight and a burden that serve no purpose other than to drive you to your knees instead of standing tall and erect and moving forward with courage and conviction, as Christ did. I try to carry my cross with dignity and courage—any less would be dishonoring those great souls who had a hand in molding me into something that I am proud to be.

The great ones who came before us in human form down through the millennia in many places in the world taught the same message. Not that they were better or greater than we are, but they travelled a road we must also travel. As they are, we will be. As we are, they once were. They shine the beacon of truth on our path that we may not stumble.

Before Gururaj underscored the truths of my faith, I was just reading words and believing what others taught me for the most part, without thinking what it really meant. My head took in the words, but it took an awakened heart to integrate them into my soul. Not only did I understand Biblical phrases anew, but I began to live them and not just talk about them.

We don't have to believe as another believes. But there's no reason for all this strife and insanity over who has the best God on the block, like there's a gang war in heaven. There's no Krishna gang against the Mohammed gang or a Mohammed gang against the Jesus gang. That picture suggests to me a West Side Story of religion, comical if it weren't so tragic.

The great originators of our religions, including Mohammed, Buddha, Christ, Krishna, and others, might just shake their heads in disbelief at some of things that have been done in their names. They might cry out, "That's not what I meant! It's like they were pointing up at the moon and saying to us all, "Look at the moon, how beautiful it is, these truths, look." And instead of looking at the moon, the truths, we look at the pointing finger.

Each of us has to sort out what we read and what we're told and make our home in the truth we find from experiencing life consciously. Life isn't in living here or there, or making a lot of money, or building great edifices. The greatest cathedral in the world, beyond all human architecture and ability, is the human heart—where Christ, Buddha, Mohammed, and Krishna live as the expressions of the divine force in human form. That force is called LOVE! They were guides; they were helpers; and they were advocates of unconditional love who went through some pretty tough times to free us from the burden of our illusions, which are the source of all suffering.

True for All or True for None

During my time with Gururaj, my understanding of truth unfolded more and more: If a truth is true, then it must be true for all people at all places at all times. True for all, or true for none. Like scientific law. Truth inviolate, invariable. It does not require time, place, or circumstance for it to be true. A God of compassion and intelligence does not make one set of rules for one group and a conflicting set of rules for another. That would be just plain stupid—AND I don't think God is stupid!

My working definition of God is like a tuning fork for me—not a dogma or a doctrine, but an expression that *unites* instead of divides, *includes* rather than excludes, *builds* instead of destroys. It gives *life* (not just physical life) instead of death and *relieves* rather than causes suffering. These are truths worthy of following and living by, or even dying for, if necessary.

CHAPTER TWELVE

My God, It's Full of Stars

How vast those Orbs must be, and how inconsiderable this
Earth, the Theater upon which all our mighty Designs, all
our Navigations, and all our Wars are transacted, is
when compared to them. — Attributed to Christiaan Huygens
(1629-1695), Dutch scientist and mathematician who proposed the
earliest theory about the nature of light

E ver since I started school after the Marine Corps and got back
into the habit of studying, I've been interested in
science—astronomy, physics, chemistry, anthropology,
paleontology, you name it. What a great joy it is to learn new things! I
always tried to see where mystical experiences fit into the relative
world of scientific thinking and known facts, even if only by indirect
inference. I've never seen anything as an isolated piece of information.
For example, truth in religion must have a corollary in the physical
universe or it doesn't make sense.

I like to connect the dots and see how things are related to each
other. I like to examine the internal wiring of life; the more wiring that
gets connected, the more I see how things relate to each other at one
level or another. Like solving a great mystery, it excites me.

'They Should Have Sent a Poet'

My process of seeing how all things are connected kicked into high
gear when I met Gururaj.

On the day before one of Gururaj's courses in England, science and spirit came together in a profound way for me.

I had a headache and wasn't feeling well. Gururaj had a healing technique that was the movement of energy in the body. He had taught several people how to do it. One fellow, Rajesh, said he'd be glad to give me a healing before lunchtime.

Our hotel was three floors, and we were on the second floor in a room that was set aside for this kind of activity. My healing session involved my lying down with eyes closed and then Rajesh would manipulate certain pressure points on my body. (Nothing unusual here if you understand things like acupressure, bioenergy, or chi.)

As he worked, I began to feel better.

Little did I know that when Rajesh began the technique, Gururaj was having lunch upstairs on the other end of the building with ten or twelve people around a big table. I was told later that all of a sudden Gururaj jumped up and walked briskly out of the lunchroom with no explanation. How he knew where to find me, I don't know; he just knew. Though my eyes were closed during the healing session, it is my personal opinion that Gururaj entered the room quietly, moved Rajesh out of the way, and took over the healing session.

Rajesh continued to speak. He asked, "Do you feel anything?"

Suddenly the normal world dropped away from me, Mr. Analytical. I was simply a point of awareness in the middle of a Hubble telescope universe. I identified with Jodie Foster's character in the film *Contact* where she witnessed a cosmic event and breathlessly said, "They should have sent a poet."

It wasn't like a dream. I was there. In three dimensions, with full color. Suns being born. Suns exploding. Galaxies moving inexorably in their dance of gravity.

My thinking mind was held in suspension. I was simply a point of observation. No body, no mind, no thought. Just witnessing. Then, all of a sudden, it was like somebody took a paintbrush and the whole scene, the whole universe, disappeared in a sheet of gold light.

The whole experience lasted only a few seconds; then I was back in my thinking mind.

I was shocked. The only words that came out of my mouth were, "My God, it's full of stars," the exact words uttered by Dave Bowman in Arthur C. Clarke's *2001: A Space Odyssey* when the monolith absorbed his spaceship.

In a few minutes, Rajesh said, "Open your eyes."

Gururaj was standing by the window in the room, just looking out.

I know that it may sound like I was hallucinating. That very well may have been. It was the next morning before I could put it into words:

"I was experiencing an ever-expanding, profound silence where that witnessing center became more and more dominant than all internal mental activity and external changing phenomena perceived by the senses. Every thought could only exist for the barest fraction of a second before disappearing. Beyond the profound silence, all manifest creations—suns, planets, the room, people, the building I was in—were moving shadows superimposed on a field of absolute silent awareness that had no edges or points of reference. The silence and movement were one—never changing and ever changing. All life was a constant and beautiful eternal dance. No death, only life changing from one form to another within that field of profound silent witnessing."

It was a peaceful and wondrous experience. After a time, the intensity subsided, but some parts are as clear today as then.

125

Once experienced, that silence and profound oneness of all creation can never be really lost. There is a subtle transformation that is forever.

The Kingdom of Heaven Within

Now, such visions are not important taken by themselves; they are more of a distraction, like a case of indigestion for which you take a Tums. The point in telling these stories is not to entertain with flashy or cool experiences, or to imply that I am unique. I'm just a regular person who works for a living and has a family, just like anyone else. I'm not different. I'm the equivalent of John Q. Public, with a few turns unique to me.

What is important to understand is that all of us are more than we believe ourselves to be, more than we can conceive of from what we have learned, what we have read, what people have told us, and all the things that make up our mental internal life or our physical external life.

I was very fortunate to have a guide, a teacher, to help point the way to me that the kingdom of heaven truly is within us. It is up to each of us to find a way to realize that which is already within all of us, and to live that oneness of harmony spontaneously more and more in our everyday lives.

Gururaj would say: "You are trying to find something that you already are. You are not going anywhere; you are just re-cognizing what you are, which was there all the time. Life takes on a richness and spontaneous unconditional love, not directed but simply present all the time. We take all these ideas of past hurts, past good things, anticipations for the future, and we let them go. If we let go of all those things that we thought were us, what is left? Only the true Self, unchanging, silent, and present at our births; it will also be there to witness the death of the body." Notice he did not say *our* bodies, because they have never belonged to us; they are only on loan. That witness will continue forever.

We are more than we believe ourselves to be. Not just this body/mind, but infinite potential, expressed as a little point in space and time. We have the ability, the potential, to perceive the entirety of "pure being" at the core of all creation. We must look for it—not on the outside, but within. We are already there. We simply have to stop being afraid of the unknown, that which spontaneously arises according to the need of the moment.

Gururaj would say that it was not his law, but the law of what is. We must sort out our own house first; only then can we begin to appreciate others or the world around us with a clear eye. Assumptions and information you take as fact or truth on hearsay from others or from books may not be true. Only what you experience directly for yourself is yours. Nobody can take that away from you or tell you it is wrong. It is your truth, validated in the crucible of your own experience.

Gururaj's teachings in a nutshell? Man, know thyself and thou knowest all things.

Energetic Forces of Creation

So much more exists than meets the eye—like an iceberg, where 10 percent is above the water line and 90 percent is below. The 10 percent of life that we see is all the movement and thoughts and actions and interactions, but the 90 percent is where the game is really played, where the more subtle energetic forces of the mind and creation are operating all of the time.

To the extent that we are in touch with and aware of the 90 percent, we are able to use those forces for our own betterment and the betterment of the world. It's not simply a matter of doing good deeds like feeding the poor or going to church. Those are all good, for sure. But how much more good could we do if we were in touch with the 90 percent below the surface and were able to draw upon those inexhaustible energies and creativity in our daily lives?

My life was about normal everyday things when I met Gururaj. Then he opened doorways and showed me possibilities that I had to explore for myself, so that I could begin to understand deeper levels of being and possibility. By natural extension, I began to have a greater appreciation for all of creation and a greater feeling for the depths of others, regardless of what was on the surface.

Theory of Everything—The Quest for Knowledge

As time passed with Gururaj, my predisposition for cosmology and my pursuit of answers to the primordial human questions grew: What power keeps the great ball of the sun in the sky? Why are there so many different things, and how can they exist in harmony without colliding or exploding in chaos?

What are the laws that allow things to manifest and express themselves? Where did the universe come from—the planets, the stars, the galaxies? Where is the universe going? That outer focus of my questioning was just a mirror image, a reflection, of my inner focus, and it seemed a very natural extension of my inner quest for knowledge or, better said, "understanding my self."

I read Stephen Hawking's *A Brief History of Time*, Albert Einstein's *Theory of Relativity*, and Sir Isaac Newton's *Principia Mathematica*, about movement, mass, and gravity. I saw this incredible cosmic dance. From this thing called a singularity (called that, apparently, because scientists don't know what the hell else to call it), this infinite point of energy, everything that can possibly be exploded, and space, time, and matter grew at a phenomenal rate. This was called the "inflationary period" where in the first few microseconds after the Big Bang, the universe of space/time sprang into existence, expanding far faster than the speed of light. (I have not gotten a handle on that one yet because, according to Einstein, nothing can go faster than the speed of light—but the universe did!)

The universe began to cool and the formation of elementary particles, atoms, and molecules formed from the homogeneous plasma, which was all that could exist in the intense temperature right after the Big Bang.

Hydrogen clumped under gravitational force until critical mass was reached and then, BOOM, the first star was born. Stars have lifetimes, just like we do; each star goes through various stages of burning heavier and heavier elements until the star runs out of fuel and either turns nova into a white dwarf or neutron star. Given sufficient mass, the star explodes into a supernova and forms a black hole. It is from these novae, basically the deaths of stars, that the universe is seeded with the heavier elements, which all life on Earth depends on for its existence. Here again we see the great circle of life—from what we call death, life springs. This is the circle of life—it exists all the way down to the most humble microbe.

The fact is that our human bodies were made billions of years ago in the hearts of stars, so we are made of star stuff. I find that absolutely amazing. It was one of those WOW moments in my life when I learned that fact.

All of these cosmological events happen within the context of scientific theories that geniuses among us continue to refine and revise. From Newton's gravity and attraction laws, to Einstein's relativity, to particle physics, quantum mechanics, and the latest kids on the block—black holes, Hawking radiation, Higgs boson particles, super symmetry, M-theory, string theory, and multiverses. It's interesting to note that Einstein tried but failed to formulate a "Theory of Everything" because he wouldn't embrace quantum theory. Stubborn old coot!

There is one specific theory that really caught my eye. This theory of the operation of matter at the quantum level incorporates the early (more than 3,500 years ago) mystics' visions of a "single wholeness of the universe" or "essential oneness" to all creation.

This theory is based on a quantum ground substrata that the mystics called "pure awareness," without content, or boundary—simply a field of awareness with the ultimate potential to become.

The theory that mathematically postulates an expression of this ultimate "oneness" of the universe in today's language of theoretical physics is called "Quantum Entanglement." Or, as Albert Einstein put it, "Spooky Action at a Distance," where one electron at one end of the universe changes its spin, and its counterpart on the other end of the universe changes instantaneously, as if there were not billions of light years intervening.

It is as if time and space at a certain quantum level do not exist, and indeed all matter exists simply as the manifest possibility of this "unified field of infinite potential." From this essence, with no time and no space, matter manifests (appearing as probability waves) in all its infinite diversity and is essentially one within this one field of pure awareness. As are we all!

Amazing that a bunch of old scruffy mystics holing up in caves 3,500 years ago cognized this reality with only their brains and meditation practices and were able to know what it took another 3,000 years and billions of research dollars to corroborate.

Here again is where science and mysticism cross paths. There are numberless other instances—if you are interested in additional material like this, I suggest *The Tao of Physics*, a book written by the physicist Fritjof Capra and published in 1975.

We Should Not Be Here!

The most phenomenal thing I discovered as I studied the origin of the Earth and humankind in general: By all accounts, we should not even be here. So many things had to be absolutely perfect in order for this planet to produce not just "life" in its lower forms like bacteria but a highly advanced technological civilization.

Life in very simple forms may exist in incredibly hostile environments; but when you are talking about sentient life—about highly technological civilizations capable of leaving the planet to study the universe and asking profound questions like how, when, and why the universe was created—that's a different kettle of fish altogether.

Consider the following:

1. It's remarkable when you consider that if the Earth weren't in this position in the solar system ninety-three million miles from our sun, life would never have arisen. It's called the Goldilocks Zone: the

right distance from the sun—not too cold, not too hot. If it were just a little different—BOOM! No Humans!

2. The Earth has a liquid iron/nickel core that spins at a thousand miles per hour creating the magnetosphere, or magnetic envelope, around the planet that keeps X-rays and solar particles from microwaving all life as we know it, and tearing away the atmosphere—like on Mars when its core cooled and water evaporated. Otherwise—BOOM! No Humans!

3. It's a fact that if the planet Jupiter were not where it is, in its precise distance from Earth with just the right orbital mechanics and mass, we probably wouldn't be here either. Jupiter has a tremendous gravitational field that sweeps up space debris. The planet acts like a cosmic vacuum cleaner before all that junk hits the inner solar system and Earth—US! Without Jupiter's gravitational field scooping up stray comets and asteroids, there would have been many more extinction-level events like the one that may have taken out the dinosaurs on Earth. Scientists are still debating that one. But some say that it took just one big rock. And whoops! There went the dinosaurs after 150 million years. It would take a far less powerful collision today, then—BOOM! No Humans.

4. Let us consider the creation of our moon and its critical gravitational effect required to keep the Earth spinning uniformly on its axis (without the moon, Earth's axis of rotation might vary as much as 90 degrees): 1. IF a proto planet had not hit the planet Earth with a glancing blow about four billion years ago at just the right offset angle to put the Earth at a 23.5 degree orbital tilt; 2. AND, IF debris from that collision had not been outside the "Roche Limit" (the minimum distance a large satellite can approach its primary body without being torn apart by tidal forces) allowing our moon to form, then, again—BOOM! No Humans!

133

5. As a result of the processes mentioned above, we get all of the basic forms of life that begin to grow and flourish and evolve through mutation. Were it not for the fact that we have just the right amount of cosmic radiation leaking through our magnetic envelope (magnetosphere), our species would not have evolved as quickly as it has and would have remained relatively static. We would not have had evolution as we know it, which is based not just on environmental conditions, but on mutation from just the right amount of cosmic radiation leaking in. And so, again—BOOM! No Humans (at least not as we know us today)!

So what does this tell us? When all factors are just right, life goes crazy. Life wants to flourish, to grow and expand and be diverse. It's magical! The incredible diversity of life came from a primordial sludge on a planet that was being bombarded by huge rocks. If you want to do some mind-blowing math, figure the odds of our being here when all the above-mentioned factors had to be in just the right place at just the right time for us to be here at all. Now if that is not called a miracle, I don't know what is.

Common Source of Matter, Energy, and Intelligence

The fact that this beautiful planet and humans can exist at all is a testament to cosmic intelligence in action.

An even more profound manifestation of this innate cosmic intelligence at work is the spontaneous emanation of energy and the precise laws of physics from the singularity that caused the Big Bang. Within that immensely violent explosion, along with unformed energy, were the laws which allowed formless energy to organize itself into systems and structures—strong nuclear force, weak nuclear force, electromagnetic force, and gravitational force—to organize energy and matter in a such way that the universe we have came into existence.

We cannot get this beautiful order that we see within the universe from chaos, without intelligence to guide the formation of higher forms and complex structures including—US! I do not care if you call this intelligence God, or natural law, or spontaneous organization. We are the ultimate expression of that intelligent design, in that we can know the essence of this intelligence within us because we are IT and its expression. We have the necessary wiring (nervous system), chemical transmitters, and physical receptors that allow us to be aware and know that we are aware—this is the definition of sentience. This physical structure gives us the possibility of experiencing pure awareness, the ultimate source of all manifest creation. How?

We turn the mind within and allow it to settle down to the point where activity gradually slows until there is only silence.

Within that silence, the mind experiences a profound sense of quietude, peace, and wholeness. We immerse the conscious mind into that unified source of energy and intelligence, which gives the conscious mind greater depth and clarity.

The expression of this sense of quietude, peace, and wholeness in our life we call love, compassion, and creativity. It is the ever-flowing fountain of all that is. Often the manifestations of this pure source get distorted into hatred, jealousy, or other negatives. We live in a world of dynamic opposites. If all at once everything was just the pure expression of love, BOOM, all creation would be over in the blink of an eye. There must be the push and pull of these energies—the Yin and Yang of life—for this universe to be. There is a reason for everything; even what we call evil has its reason for being.

The fact that we exist, and that we've learned so much in such a short period of time, is a testament to the potential that is within humankind, within each one of us.

All things are connected; everything is truly one in its essence and, at the same time, coexistent with its polar opposite; otherwise,

everything would blow up and go haywire. This is the paradox that verifies there is some higher intelligence beyond all the names and forms continually in operation. It must exist, for if it did not, like matter and anti-matter canceling each other out, so would all opposing energies simply cancel each other out in the blink of an eye. They don't because intelligence is acting at a fundamental level such that all opposites can co-exist in harmony.

Everything Is One

So my study of cosmology, physics, chemistry, anthropology, and different philosophical schools keeps pointing in the same direction: Everything is one. It is pure being, or existence, appearing as many forms.

Paradoxical but true. Many cells. Many thoughts. Many different functions, but essentially one whole organism within one universe. Ultimately, at the level of "being" or "pure awareness," there is no difference between the furthest galaxy and me. All the elements that make up this body were forged from stardust billions of years ago. My existence and the existence of the furthest galaxy is the same. Only outer appearances are different, not the essence.

This consciousness or awareness—the foundation within this body/mind construct—is the same for this entire space/time universe and all the multiverses that exist or ever will exist. Isn't that phenomenal?

Mind boggling. Incredible complexity and incomprehensible beauty and, at the same time, elegant simplicity. And it all comes down to one thing—pure, uncompounded awareness, whose nature it is to manifest in form, exist in form, for a brief time, then merge back into that primordial awareness (or energy). It is the endless cycle of silence and motion, potential and kinetic energy, which is the eternal engine of creation.

Highly improbable you may say. But look, we're here! Our own existence and observation of the universe around us demonstrate that there is a continuous cycle of birth, change, and dissolution—the eternal dance of Shiva and Shakti (silence and activity). Everything follows the same eternal cycle over and over again throughout eternity. We are such marvelous creatures in such a marvelous universe.

Yes, there is suffering and pain, just as we experience pleasure, joy, and happiness. But at the source—the center, the silent balance point—the weather is calm.

Gururaj had his arguments with philosophers like René Descartes who said, "I think, therefore I am." Gururaj would say, "I am, therefore I think!"

Gururaj used to say that Western philosophy, as such, says much but goes nowhere—circle talk! It never gets to the punch line!

It's only when we get stuck in the clatter of energy in our minds and around us that we get lost. We identify ourselves with all of the separate thoughts and forms instead of stopping, turning within, and becoming quiet so that radiant, beautiful awareness can shine forth in its full glory within us. But we must take the first steps toward inner exploration.

It is necessary for us to turn within and combine the outer forms of life with that inner pure awareness, so that only the great single harmony of life exists, where all parts of our life, both inner and outer, are in balance. The outcome is that our life becomes the expression of "the peace that passeth all understanding." That's my story anyway, and I am sticking to it!

CHAPTER THIRTEEN

Be Yourself!
Be Your True Self!

The beginning of love is to let those we love be perfectly
themselves, and not to twist them to fit our own image.
Otherwise we love only the reflection of ourselves we find in
them. — from *No Man Is an Island*, a book by Thomas Merton (1915-
1968), Trappist Monk, Our Lady of Gethsemani Abbey, Kentucky

I t's hard to put into words. Most people saw Gururaj when he was
being the guru. I'd see him in the morning when he got up and his
hair in forty thousand different directions, his teeth out, in his
pajamas and slippers. I always looked worse than he did. Both of us
looked like we were chewed up and spit out, or someone had stuck our
heads in a blender—too awful to imagine!

One afternoon I walked into the bedroom at our house where he
was taking a nap. I had the most bizarre feeling. I saw this body on a
bed. It was curled up and snoring. But that little form meant absolutely
nothing. It was like a thin transparency of tissue paper. Beyond that
body was an intense presence that filled the room, an intangible
awareness. No words. No thoughts. No feelings. Just intense
awareness and the sound of a sleeping man.

The body was a shell that contained a pure awareness of incredible
power, scope, and depth. It was solid, like walking into a room where
the air had coalesced into something palpable. But it had no boundary

and no edges. And I could feel it emanating from this silly little form lying on the bed. That really threw me for a loop.

As I washed my face, he woke up.

He came around the bed and took me by the shoulders, shook me, and said, "Be Yourself! Be your True Self!"

He yelled with incredible intensity for more than a minute.

"Wake the hell up, for God's sake! You are not what you think you are. Not this bundle of thoughts and emotions and history. Not this imaginary Bob Anderson. Not this limited set of concepts you believe yourself to be. Nor this body that came into this world and is going to leave it! You are more! Wake up!"

That rattled me. I wasn't scared, but it was almost like someone shaking a building to its foundations. Then I walked on out of the bedroom.

What in the World Did I Throw Away?

Some profound experiences occurred when Gururaj and I were not even together. I'd just be at home, walking around or brushing my teeth. There would be a flash when all of the pieces lined up, and everything for a brief moment was exactly the way it should be. Everything wore the mask of something underneath it. It was an indefinable something that was the same in all things. It was a sense of the "real" behind the appearance of the shape or event. The moments when it all lined up were not frequent, nor did they last long, but were very intense and solidified within me the absolute assurance that this solid "reality" of pure awareness was undeniable.

My own experience made that conviction rock solid and will never change. The most important thing that these experiences reinforced was: "To thine own self be true." That which you personally experience is yours forever.

I'll never forget one time in particular.

It happened during a course I was taking in the UK with Gururaj and Vidya. I got up in the morning, just like I normally do, and was going to a late morning talk by Gururaj.

I was minding my own business. I ate breakfast and had a cup of coffee. All of a sudden the world of form and shape began to recede from my immediate field of waking consciousness. The world of name and form didn't go away, but something else began to push into the foreground. That which was pushing forward was an overwhelming silence and a sense of something indescribably "real." This realness was absolutely silent but was diamond-hard in its reality and clarity. Pure awareness was dominant within my mind; the material world appeared to become less substantial as this awareness pushed into my conscious mind.

Throughout the morning, the experience kept getting more intense. The body was walking and talking. I would hear words coming out of the mouth, but I was neither the words nor the one talking. No thoughts could be sustained. A thought would arise, but in the moment of its arising it would immediately disappear into the silence again. The silence swallowed everything. Every thought, feeling, and movement existed for the moment, and then everything flattened out once again into that silence. It was so powerful that I was unable to recognize "me" within the experience.

The merest ghost of a thought flashed through my mind, "There's nothing to do. It's all complete. Everything is complete even as it arises. No need to do anything." It was not apathy. No, it was seeing the absolute perfection in everything that came into the field of this awareness, whether a thought from the mind or an external sound or form. Everything was perfect as it was, as that essential complete silence of awareness. A thought flashed through the mind (not *my* mind), "My goodness, I can't go to work and raise a family like this. Nothing needs to be done. It is all perfect as it is."

There is no way I could sit in an office and go through the mundane motions amid this huge silence, awareness, and presence.

I went to Gururaj's room, where he was sitting on the bed having a cup of tea before his talk. I didn't say a word. I knelt beside the bed and put my head on his knee. Without discussion, he began wiping his hand over my brow. Every time he moved his hand across my forehead it was like somebody had pulled the plug in a tub and the silence began to recede. After about four or five times, the old personality and memories more or less were back in place.

Many, many times since I have wondered, "What in the world did I throw away?" In effect, I asked to have something taken away that most people spend a lifetime searching for, going through tremendous austerities to realize. It was handed to me on a silver platter, and I threw it away. It never came back, except in brief flashes from time to time, perhaps as a reminder of what fear can do to limit our perception and awareness. This fleeting experience was a most supremely peaceful time. I didn't see things fragmented, or as disassociated objects. Everything was whole and complete.

Oh Shit, I'm Busted!

One day after work, I went out with some friends and smoked some pot. I had a nice little buzz going but nothing big. I had smoked pot when I was much younger, but I had to quit—not for moral reasons, but because it irritated my lungs, which had a predisposition toward asthma.

Gururaj was absorbed in creating a painting at the kitchen table when I walked into the house that evening, and saw me start toward the stairs. He said to me, "Suj, how's it going?" Then, without waiting for my response, he got a quizzical look on his face, cocked his head to one side, and said, "Suj, what's wrong with you?"

"What do you mean? I'm fine," I said.

He said, "Your mind is fuzzy."

I'm thinking, "Oh shit, I'm busted." I swear, as the Lord is my witness, Gururaj could see through me like I was a cheap newspaper. He could pick my thought forms out of thin air.

Steak and Eggs and Bloody Marys

My friend Harry Hall was and is one of the most devoted members of the entire AMS organization, though he doesn't make a big deal of it. He has selflessly given countless hours of work toward administrative tasks, while his wife, Stella (Sutriya), has been focused on the preservation of the Guru's audio and video files. They joined Gururaj's circle several years after Vidya and I did.

Harry and I became fast friends.

Maybe I'm just a bit of an anarchist at heart, or iconoclast. What everybody else is doing I go out of my way NOT to do. Maybe that explains why Harry and I would have steak and eggs and Bloody Marys for breakfast while attending AMS courses, and we'd be half lit by the time we got back for Gururaj's talks. I'd go to the back of the room and fall asleep and start snoring. Gururaj never said a word nor would he allow anyone else to disturb me. Not once. He looked into the heart of a person, not just what appeared on the surface. He loved me unconditionally. He did not try to change me—to teach, to advise, but never to mandate. I grew. I changed…in my time, in my own way, on my own terms—not from fear or guilt or on someone else's terms.

143

Another person whom I met at a meditation course Gururaj conducted in 1979 was Lee Swanson. He and I hit it off immediately and have been as close as brothers ever since. When I met Lee he was operating his mail-order business out of his garage. He asked me to come to Fargo and help turn his rolodex card system into a computerized order processing and shipping system. Today his business is a hugely successful nationwide distributor of high-quality, low-cost healthcare products. We've been hanging out together and traveling all over the world ever since. My mom calls him "son number two." We take care of each other; we are family. I love Lee as though he were a blood brother. What defines a true friend or brother is unconditional love.

The Inner Guru

Gururaj delivered eternal truths that changed my life, but none more important than the idea of the inner guru, the inner teacher. He told me one evening, "I am nothing but the expression you called into being."

"What?" I asked.

He said that the inner guru—that inner Truth, which is the life of all existence—radiates what is needed to bring things into a state of balance no matter where in the universe. Whether it's a pea, a stone, a human, a planet, a galaxy, or the universe is irrelevant. That impulse, in spiritual terms, is what people call the Satguru (true or highest teacher) within, the supreme teacher that draws into our environment what we need to unfold our true potential and wake up from the web of dreams we have caught ourselves in. It is we who determine what we draw into our lives, consciously or unconsciously. The universe does not care, other than it seeks to balance the equation—call it action/reaction, call it karma, or anything else, a rose by any other name smells just as sweet.

"If a physical guru is required, then one appears. If a physical guru is not required, then something else will be there," Gururaj said.

"Everything that appears, whether it's a person, a situation, a physical ailment, whatever—nothing is by accident. Everything happens according to a purpose. And it is the purpose of that inner guru to simply remove the veils of illusion that we have placed in front of our own eyes believing that this world is what is real, when, in fact, this world is what is unreal because of its ever-changing nature."

The Real is a sphere of unchanging pure being or awareness within us. The unreal changes—it comes into form, exists for a while, then dissolves. By definition, the Real cannot change. This pure awareness was the same at the beginning of creation, remains the same throughout the cycles and eons of change, and will remain unchanged when all creation dissolves.

Think of some individual, some illness, or some painful situation and ask, "Why did this have to happen?" We cannot understand the "why" of it, because we can't see all the energy dynamics that are going on within the person and the environment. All the energies (thought, emotion, actions) are interacting the way they must, but not in a way our intellect and limited mind can understand.

We think we are the doers, or prime movers, of the action—and it is our personal ego that identifies itself with the action and its outcome. There's where we get ourselves messed up. We are the experiencers of the doing, but we are not the prime initiators of the doing. Doing happens spontaneously and automatically in response to our mental concepts, conditioning, and external influences and dynamics—all the energies interacting both within us and outside of us.

As we learn to relax into observing and allowing things to unfold as they must, our lives become smoother. We are happier and more at peace because we're not in conflict with this person, that person, this thought, or that concept. We allow everything to be as it is. It is there for a reason, though we may not know what it is. This does not mean that we are passive and just allow things to happen randomly or chaotically. WE ACT TO THE BEST OF OUR ABILITY AND RESOURCES! Plan, by all means. Work hard, by all means. But work selflessly and let go of the outcome.

It is self-delusion that we control our lives or that we control circumstances. The more we attach ourselves to that illusion of control, the more we suffer when the outer world shows us that we are not in control. Unfortunately these lessons are very painful as our personal illusions are torn away from us.

When life gets stuck in expectations of results and projections for the future and the outcome continues to be out of sync with our desire, THAT defines *suffering*. When we let go of expectations and fantasies, life flows freely and effortlessly, and THAT defines *peace*.

Fargo, North Dakota

Gururaj was giving talks at a private home. He was playing the fool, and it seemed to me being very nasty to the lady who was our host.

I kept thinking, "This is wrong. This is over the edge. I'm out of here."

So I left the house we were in and walked around the neighborhood for half an hour. I had decided I was done with all this crap. I was going back home. My wife could do whatever, but I was finished.

I got back to the house expecting to tell my wife and Gururaj that I was leaving, and there was Gururaj lying on the floor like he was dying, gasping for air. Vidya was bending over him in a state of panic. It was like the guy was having a coronary. I immediately snapped out of my pissed-off mode and jumped into a how-do-I-fix-this mode.

"What do I do now, call 911?" I said to myself. I knew he had a heart condition.

"Bapuji, what's wrong, what are you feeling?"

He looked up to me with tears in his eyes and rolling down his face, and said, "Why forsakest thou me?" (I had never said a word to him about leaving.)

In that instant, it was as if these words echoed from an incredibly distant time and life (though I do not particularly believe in past lives). I could remember being with another master and jumping ship when things got tough—now, this might have been some hallucination from something I ate or rerunning a scene from an old movie. Who knows? Regardless of the origin, Gururaj's words echoed in my heart and mind. At that moment, all the anger went away, and I knew that no matter how goofy things got or crazy things were, I would never desert him. I completely surrendered to the power of the divine when I said to myself, "I don't care what happens anymore. Maybe sometime in another lifetime I might have left, but I wasn't going to do it again."

I was kneeling next to him and had not said a word to him aloud, but it was at the moment when I made that silent decision that he began to stir, then get up (though a little wobbly). After about thirty minutes, all was back to normal.

Fire in the Silence

We were in England. Vidya and some others went to a concert or play. I was tired and I did not want to go. Gururaj didn't want to go, either. We were staying in this old English house. Gururaj was reading in his room.

It was chilly and there was a fireplace and wood in the living room. I built a nice big fire and it was crackling away. I was sitting in front of

the fire, and off to the side I saw the light from his room as he opened the door and came down the stairs. He didn't say anything. He sat in a big overstuffed leather chair next to the fireplace. Everything was dark except for the fire.

Again, I experienced one the most supremely satisfying moments of my life. I was sitting next to his chair on the floor. I laid my head on his knee. He was stroking his hand through my hair…an affectionate gesture. We didn't say anything for some time.

Then he said, "You see how those sparks separate themselves from the fire. They exist for a moment and then fall back into the fire. That's the human soul. It seems to separate from the fire of the divine, but it really doesn't. It seems to exist in form for only the tiniest fraction of time and then goes back into the divine fire, all natural in the circle of existence."

He and I were the only ones there in the dark. No lamps. Just the fire, with the shadows on the walls of the dancing flames. We just sat there watching the fire for an hour or so. I would stir the fire occasionally. Then I'd return to sit by his chair and put my head on his knee.

Sitting in the quiet, dark room, it was so peaceful, I felt like a warrior who had taken his armor off and didn't have to face another battle. Just for the moment, I didn't have to fight. I was at peace.

This is only one example of Gururaj's loving presence that was continuous even when we were separated by many miles. He and I wrote letters back and forth. They speak to all of us, not just to one of us. I've included some of them in Appendix B at the end of the book.

CHAPTER FOURTEEN

Everything We Need Is Within Us

Thought is the mother of action. And if our thinking, if our minds are permeated by that divine energy, then automatically our thinking becomes unlabored and spontaneous. In that spontaneity there is a beautiful rightness where we flow with the current of nature and not against the current of nature. — Gururaj Ananda Yogi

All things happen for a reason. Nothing happens by accident. Whether hard knocks or good things, there is a reason and a time for all things. When we accept both—the great wonderful things and the sorrowful things—with a sense of equanimity, we stop being at the mercy of the mind and emotions and live a life of greater balance, of greater harmony. This does not mean that we do not feel, laugh, or cry—absolutely not. BUT the important thing is that we do not hold on to these emotions or memories, that we live in the present moment. Yes, feel sorrow or happiness for some event, but then let it go and flow with life—so that you are not stuck in past memories or emotions. When we live in the NOW of each moment, in the flow of life, we are not banged over and over again into the same rocks.

We are the silent witness to the balance point at the center around which all our thoughts, feelings, our life and indeed all creation revolve. We are that! All of us!

We have everything that we need within us—built in—to go to the farthest edges of consciousness, beyond the universe, to be able to know anything we need to know at the right time. Just by deepening our connection with our own inner self, we touch the wellspring where all knowledge resides in its quiet form. When we get into circumstances where we need some knowledge to do something, if we listen to that still voice within—not simply our mental concepts or our feelings of fear and anxiety—something will come to us that's appropriate to the moment. I've never found it to fail me. Not once.

That doesn't mean I walk around going ohmmmmm. I've never walked around with a soft-spoken voice. I get angry, but not for long. I can't hold on to anger. I can't hold a grudge. Perhaps I can hold on to garbage for an hour or two, or maybe a day if I work at it. But that's about it. It takes too much energy to hold onto anger, regret, or jealousy. It's not been something I tried to do. It happened more or less gradually and naturally over time (years) where negative emotions simply would not stick in the mind or memory. They might flash into the mind, but there was no energy given to them to sustain their continued existence, and they simply dissolved. No effort was involved; the mind was simply re-patterned so these thoughts and emotions had no place to live.

What is the personal benefit of re-patterning our mind? The benefit is that we are at peace. Peace is silence, no conflicting emotions, no crowding thoughts to bring confusion, no suffering. We become the personal expression of "the balance point" where all is motionless, until some action is required. The necessary action happens, then silence once again, until something else is needed. As the Apostle Paul called it, "The peace that passeth all understanding" (Philippians 4:7). That is our natural state—peace that is real, solid. The rock-solid peace of the lively silence within our heart and mind is there if we let go of the past, stop conjuring up some fictional future that will probably not happen, and live in the present moment, in the NOW of life.

I wasn't running around looking for a guru when I came to know Gururaj. I was living my life, doing TM, and quite satisfied, except that I still had that internal drive to reach out beyond where I was in terms of understanding and unfolding potential. That was always in the background. So it's not that I went looking for a teacher. Almost the reverse happened. The teacher was in search of me, but not from the ego point of view. According to Gururaj's teachings, when someone is truly open or yearning for greater knowledge of self or God, that personal relationship—that love affair with the divine—then the universe will manifest and bring into our sphere of life what is needed to fulfill that desire.

We have the power to manifest in our lives anything that we truly, truly desire that is not selfish, that is selfless, earnest, steadfast, and focused; I guarantee you absolutely, 100 percent without a doubt it will happen. I know this for a fact because it has happened in my own life time and again.

I would simply ask anyone who is listening or reading to sit quietly and consider this: Open the mind and heart to possibilities, because we are infinitely possible if we only allow ourselves the space to be more than we think we are. When we drop our burdens and accept the gifts that are waiting at our doorsteps, we are able to reach beyond our present condition. We are able to enlist courage and open our hearts enough to let go of our preconceived concepts of the world, people, and how the divine plan works.

How do we do that? Pray, go to church, meditate, study, read, be with people of good character, offer our life continually to grace. Go within! Find some way to quiet down the mind to get to a spot where the divine light that is ever shining within us has the room to shine up through the mind and out into our lives. If we are always stuck in the mind, in fixed mental concepts, in the past or in the future, how can the divine light shine through all that muck? How is it possible?

We are stuck in a prison of our own making and we have to take it apart brick by brick, just like we created it, until divine light can shine through the mind in its full glory and out to the world. So many great souls have done this throughout human history. Why can't we take lessons from them? Not from one person and one place at one time, but from all the great souls of all times and places throughout human history, for they have a common message. They spoke in the same language, the language of love, that we are one, not separate pieces fragmented and alone. But within the depth of the heart or soul, whatever you wish to call it, we are all one: brothers and sisters of the same Father. No matter what robes we put on or what culture we come from. No matter what color of skin, eyes, and hair.

Underneath, the same Father of us all—loving, giving, ever merciful—is trying, gently if possible but sternly if necessary, to guide us through our own adolescence and limitations to a wider world, a wider sense of possibility, a wider appreciation of what is always around us and within us.

The Self of All, Not the Self of One

I journeyed with Gururaj for twelve years. I always try to be worthy of what he taught and his tireless effort on my behalf. He taught unstintingly, unwaveringly, with unconditional love and great patience and by example. I watched how he was with people. I saw how he worked himself to death in service to others. He did not seek great accolades or worship. He had very little money, barely enough to keep him and his family in bread and beans. That's who and what he was. He couldn't help it. It was his nature. As he would say, "True realization is when we are in touch with our true self. It is selfless and in service to all. There is the paradox. When we are in touch with our true self, it is the self of all, not the self of one."

Till the day this body dies (not I), I will do my best to live up to the ideal that Gururaj demonstrated by hard work in his daily life—to help everyone see a wider horizon and to find a true sense of the real Self. He saw beyond the personal ego; he communicated to the real Self within that is the Self of all. Only when this True Self is realized can we truly love unconditionally—when we see all as "my" self.

When I see myself as separate from everyone, how is it possible for me to truly love? When my so-called love is always conditioned on something, that is not love, but bargaining, or shop keeping—you do this for me and I will love you; if you don't, I will withdraw my love. How many times have we seen this within others or ourselves? Let's be honest. How many times have we given love or friendship only to withdraw it if a person doesn't meet our expectations? Again, this is not real love, but false love born out of selfishness or insecurity. Unconditional love flows openly without restriction, condition, or motive and requires nothing in return.

During the twelve years I knew him, I never once saw Gururaj act out of selfishness, out of a sense of, "Look at me, I'm hot stuff." Not once! Unless he was delivering some kind of teaching that someone needed. Somehow he always knew exactly what each person needed.

For twelve years, I experienced some of the most terrifying, in some ways, and some of the most wonderful years of my life—growing beyond my boundaries and getting rid of preconceived notions and ideas. I learned, at least to some degree, to live with a sense of evenness when things went well and also when things did not. Not stoically, but with understanding. I do not think anyone could ever receive any greater gift than understanding and peace.

CHAPTER FIFTEEN

A Call from South Africa

As water in the ocean rises and swells into the shape of a wave,
flows for a while and then falls back into the ocean,
without ever for a moment being anything other than
water, so every object, every experience, arises within
Consciousness, takes its unique shape, does its unique
thing, and then offers back its name and form to the
ocean of Presence, which abides in and as itself, before
taking the shape of the next wave. — Rupert Spira, ceramic
artist and seeker, from his book *The Transparency of Things,
Contemplating the Nature of Experience* (2008)

Gururaj told us that we would no longer need the outer guru
when the connection to our own inner guru was established in
our hearts. But few, if any, of us truly believed that we had
reached that level of internal communion when we waved goodbye to
him in Canada on Easter in 1988.

Just a few weeks later, on May 17, 1988, I was at work in
Allentown, Pennsylvania, when my wife phoned.

"I just got a call from South Africa," Vidya said.

Bapuji had died suddenly of a heart attack.

The story that was told to Vidya was that the day before he died he
got dressed up in his best suit and tie. Very sharp. He visited his

children, grandchildren, and closest friends. He didn't say goodbye per se, but it must have been on his mind and in his heart.

A couple of days before he died he had called us. I spoke to him briefly, not knowing at the time that it would be the last time I would talk to him in a physical body.

None of us in the worldwide circle of his students went to the funeral. He was cremated within three days.

It hit me very hard. It was heart wrenching and incredibly sad. How would any of us feel when father, friend, and confidant—someone who exemplified all of those things that you were striving for—was gone physically?

People said, "Yes, yes, but he'll always be there in the spirit, always guiding." It wasn't the same for me. No matter what anybody said, I didn't care—for me it was a tremendous personal loss. I couldn't have a scotch with him, put my arm around him, have a cigarette with him. Or listen to his bad jokes. Or lay my weary head down on his knee.

OK, so I'm not all that evolved. I was attached to a physical person. I can live with that.

It took me quite a while to get over Gururaj's death, but as with all of life, you move on. I tried to take what I had learned and continue to learn and grow in my own way, the best I knew how—the way he taught me, by putting one foot in front of the other. I guess, in a weird sort of way, I wanted to make my father proud. That may sound silly, but it means a lot to me. I would never betray Gururaj; I would never do anything to cast a shadow on him or his teachings, because he was just too precious to me.

CHAPTER SIXTEEN

Recovery from a Career Crash

As long as we're caught up in always looking for certainty and
  happiness, rather than honoring the taste and smell and
  quality of exactly what is happening, as long as we're always
  running from discomfort, we're going to be caught in a cycle
  of unhappiness and discomfort, and we will feel weaker and
  weaker. This way of seeing helps us develop inner strength.
  And what's especially encouraging is the view that inner
  strength is available to us at just the moment when we think
  that we've hit the bottom, when things are at their worst. —
  Pema Chödrön, an American Buddhist Nun in the Tibetan Tradition, in
  her book *Practicing Peace in Times of War* (2006)

I had been incredibly successful at Revlon, and had begun to think
I was pretty cool. Limousines picked me up. I stayed at the Plaza
Hotel on Fifth Avenue in New York City. And I had a reserved
parking space at the home office. I was a fairly young executive in my
thirties with all the trappings of success—on top of the world
financially and professionally.

I always had the idea that I had to work harder than anybody else to
compensate for not having all the pedigrees other successful people
seemed to have. So, working many hours a day, I did well. I tripled
my salary during my ten years as Group Director of Management

Information Services for Revlon Health Care, Pharmaceutical Division. I managed all information technology activities for five companies within the division.

I worked my butt off on high-visibility projects and had the grace of God and a lot of good people working with me. The gang and I would consistently pull the chestnuts out of the fire. The eyes of the entire corporation focused on us. I was project manager and principal engineer for one of the Health Care Groups' major Order Processing and Inventory Control Systems. They were incredibly complex and had calculations and tracking that included drug potencies, half-lives, and shelf lives of certain chemicals, and, of course, Food and Drug Administration (FDA) lot recall capability. In addition, there were components that tracked all of the different contractual agreements and pricing variations we had with wholesalers. On time and within budget, I demoed the new system to the senior technology executives of the Health Care Group. It was an instant success. My personal stock soared, and I was in playing with the big boys.

Revlon had been the best part of my career to that point.

Losing Job After Job

I met Gururaj during my career rise from Armour to Revlon. So, he was alive to witness that career highpoint. During our relationship, I intellectually learned many spiritual truths, but I had not fully integrated them within when job loss struck in 1986.

That year, Revlon was the target of a hostile takeover in one of the first junk bond rearrangements originally engineered by the infamous Michael Milken. He and his partners sold off all the individual companies and assets of the Revlon Health Care Group in order to service the debt on the purchase of Revlon Cosmetics. In the process, they made a fortune, but also ruined so many lives. In the movie *Wall Street* when actor Michael Douglas, portraying corporate raider

Gordon Gekko, said that "greed, for lack of a better word, is good," it may have meant that greed makes money, but from my perspective, it sure as hell ain't good. I lost my job at Revlon. My universe changed suddenly, dramatically, and painfully.

When you lose a job and you have a wife and kids and a mortgage, it's terrifying. Colleen and Crystal were about ten and twelve years old.

In my first attempt to bounce back, I wound up going with a company in Pennsylvania, against Gururaj's advice, by the way.

I moved the family from Bourbonnais in Illinois to Fort Washington in Pennsylvania.

Unfortunately, I didn't understand the politics at the new company, and I didn't have the same latitude to get things done that I'd had in my previous job, so within a year I was let go.

My family and I endured several job losses and moves in the following years. Vidya was a school psychologist and had to change jobs every time we moved. During this time, she earned her doctorate in school psychology and continued to teach meditation. Packing and unpacking in house after house in new towns became a way of life. Our daughters had to acclimate to one school after another. This time of upheaval was devastating to me and terribly hard on Vidya, Colleen, and Crystal, but it put my career life into perspective.

Naturally this was a fertile time for my spiritual life. We never know what we have learned or integrated within until it is put to the test, sometimes in a very hard way. We always get what we need; the universe does not make mistakes nor is it cruel. We simply lack the perspective and breadth of vision to see what is really needed for us to grow as fully integrated human beings. I needed the failures or, better said, "hard lessons." I thought I was hot stuff. I was the kingpin, then without warning everything that used to work, didn't. These may have been necessary personal lessons, but to be honest, I would rather have had a poke in the eye with a sharp stick. This time of my life really sucked!

It was the universe trying to teach me a tough lesson: You are not your job or what you do. Don't get puffed up when things go well, and always be prepared to hit bottom if they don't.

It took a while, but finally I began to realize that our abilities come to us as a gift and a blessing. A saying goes, "To work you have the right, but not to the fruits thereof; that belongs to God" (*Bhagavad Gita*, 2nd Chapter, 47th verse). What that means is that when you think you are "the doer," then your ego identifies itself with the outcome. When the outcome is good, your ego puffs up; when the outcome is bad, you suffer. Therefore, work for the sake of work, for the love of the work. Do your best and what happens after that is not your concern. We cannot know all the different energies that are interacting that determine the final outcome. Be at peace with yourself, knowing that you did the best you could, given the circumstances, and after that, what happens will happen. The results of action have to be exactly what they are, or they would have been something else. When you become enamored of yourself remember…pride cometh before the fall.

Let me tell you—I fell big time and hit rock bottom HARD.

My "job" lessons from the universe resulted in a greater internal understanding of spiritual principles because I then had firsthand experience of exactly what they meant. I learned that what appeared on the surface to be misfortune was really the greatest blessing in disguise. The greatest lesson for me was, "Never fight with what IS, because IS always wins." AND, you are not what you do! Do your best; then let go of the outcome.

I became conscious of my basic faith and trust in the power of the universe that it knows what it's doing. Though I may not fully understand, I trust that when anything that appears stressful happens, it's for a purpose, and there's something I need to learn. Suffering is a call to action, a call to investigate within and see what is causing the suffering. The universe simply readjusted my perspective, and with this realignment came the realization that the world did not revolve around me—it was time to grow up, and this had nothing to do with my chronological age.

Job of My Dreams

In 1988, after the anxiety of several years of one job loss after another, plus the intense grief over Gururaj's death, an opportunity arose that signaled a recovery from my career crash and the next big chapter of my life.

I reached out to a young, vibrant, and growing company—Computer Aid, Inc., or CAI—which was recommended to me by a consultant I worked with. It was a computer and technology consulting firm that in 1988 had about $10 million a year in sales and about 300 employees. I met the owner and president, Tony Salvaggio, at Chi-Chi's Mexican restaurant where he interviewed me over margaritas and chips. I got just a little buzzed, but Tony offered me a job that initially took me on the road as a consulting analyst (which I had not done for many years). I was very happy to be employed. I found the company's entrepreneurial spirit very exciting.

Almost twenty-five years later, my relationship with Tony as a friend and mentor has grown and enriched both my personal and professional life. Tony, like Gururaj, accepted me for what I was—guess he saw some potential that later bore considerable fruit for both myself and Computer Aid.

Tony Salvaggio

Tony, like Gururaj, is someone who trusts me and puts up with me. I'm one intense individual, very strong in my opinions about things. He is ever so tolerant. It's hard to describe Tony—he's probably one of the most brilliant and best human beings I know in this world and he happens to be my boss. Tony is like a guardian angel and probably one of just a few people for whom I would crawl through a minefield filled with broken glass chips. We do not socialize, but he is almost like a brother to me. I always watch his back and he always watches mine.

I work as hard as I always have, but Tony runs circles around me, keeping a schedule that would pound me into the ground like a nail. He is always positive and encouraging, honest, and leads with great personal integrity.

Tony founded CAI in 1981 to provide information technology services to companies of all sizes. Then, as now, in most business organizations, many IT projects were hampered by missed deadlines, poor quality, and budget overruns. CAI fills a critical niche, addressing these issues by developing repeatable processes and procedures that form the backbone of the consulting services we provide.

To put it simply, we offer a recipe for IT success for CAI and our client companies.

In 1988, as I began work in the consulting division of CAI, I would go into one of our corporate client's business systems environment with our application support team—for a fee—and eventually that service would turn out to be a large part of CAI's revenue. The CAI consulting team and I would learn our clients' business structures, application systems, and how their operations worked. We consulted with our customers in a way that we looked invisible to the application users; we looked like their own company employees, only doing a better job than their previous team had done.

The first big job I tackled was to maintain billing applications for DuPont. Then, customer by customer, I began to write everything down. I tracked how we did things that worked and improved our service performance. What did we have to look out for that might cause problems? Little by little, I compiled a complete operations manual for supporting our customers' software applications.

Tony immediately saw that documenting processes made sense. He gave me a small budget to start. When we delivered, he gave me a little more money and finally enough funding over time to get the job done. So, over a fifteen-year period, we wrote ten software operational process guides. Along the way, we also developed training courses to match the technical operations process guides. We created training CDs, started a training department, and developed a print shop to handle production of all the training material, process guides, and sales materials.

Our Process Development and Training Department became an integral part of Computer Aid's service offerings. It started with a half-time typist and me. I was beginning to realize, however, that once an idea is out there it takes on a life of its own.

We built this line of business from nothing to where it is today, significant revenue measured in many millions of dollars annually with high profit and a constant annuity revenue stream through multi-year contracts (annuity means the money keeps rolling in month after month for the life of the contract).

Nothing happens in isolation. During this time more spiritual realizations accompanied the creative work I was doing for CAI. Remember, we are whole beings—what affects one area of our lives has an impact on all other areas of our lives, for good or ill.

Knowledge Coming Through Me Not From Me

The beauty of it was that all this knowledge wasn't coming from me; it was coming through me. I didn't feel that "I" was creating something. I didn't have that sense of ego that I was the doer or creator of outcomes. During my career crisis, I had the opportunity to have that bashed out of me pretty thoroughly. At CAI, it was just fun to create. I would watch, almost like a bystander, as these ideas and thoughts would come flooding out and take on a life of their own. It seemed all I had to do was think of something and the universe would automatically bring everything that was needed at just the right time. I never knew how things would turn out, I just did the best job I knew how out of love for the job and love for Tony and the company. Everything else took care of itself.

A tremendous sense of joy accompanied the process of watching that happen without thinking that I was doing it. It was doing itself and I was watching! When I had the attitude—just to love doing for the sake of doing something creative—I was infused with the joy of creating something from pure thought and all of a sudden something manifested in the outer world. Things worked smoothly and harmoniously. People were happy and less stressed; they had a handle on their work environment. I was participating in a beautiful dance.

165

Tracer—Process Control and Software Engineering

I decided one day in 1997 that it would be neat if we had a way to automate CAI's processes like the process control systems used to measure the efficiency of a manufacturing operation—like whether you are spending time wisely and creating the product according to specifications. This idea came into my head and, with my eyes closed, I could see the pieces coming together out of nothing, like a vision. If it could be done, it would complete the life cycle of process management, data collection, and performance measurement to support business applications for our customers. Most importantly, our competitors did not have anything like this. It was an exciting concept.

I talked to Tony about it.

"What if we were able to take application support processes and combine them with certain business rules that say you have to do this and this and this before you can do this? And what if we put our measurement points inside the work processes and then track all the work, resources, deadlines, time, and service commitments with measurement reports to see how well we were delivering CAI service? Wouldn't that be cool?"

Tony said, "Try it. You can have the time of some people whose work isn't directly billable. See what you can create and then get back to me."

I was still consulting on customer sites, so more nights and weekends were required. The interesting thing is that many other people in CAI volunteered their nights and weekends with me to develop the prototype of this new system. I never asked them to work extra—I shared the vision and they ran with it.

We called the new system "Tracer" because it could trace work resources, effort, quality, and measurements. It seemed like a good name at the time.

It took fourteen months before the first version of CAI's process management, event tracking, and resource management system was ready to try in a customer engagement at AMP in Harrisburg, Pennsylvania.

Tracer and our defined processes for application support account for a significant part of the company's revenue and profit.

Although I was the initial sparkplug, once the Tracer team got the vision, they started coming up with ideas, and it was out of my hands. It had a life of its own. Tracer is patented, with me as the inventor, though I simply started the snowball rolling down the hill. A lot of smart people blessed with insight expressed their own creativity. Then doggone, if it didn't work! Then we all just had a good time.

I'm good at generating ideas and blessed with communicating enthusiasm, but so is everybody else if you give them a chance.

In December 2009, the United States Patent and Trademark Office issued a Patent Certificate with this description:

SYSTEM AND METHOD FOR PROCESS AUTOMATION AND ENFORCEMENT
In process automation, processes are entered and enforced on team members through a Web interface. Processes are selected from a process library and can be updated as needed. Governance algorithms guide team members in carrying out the processes. The Web interface comprises a dashboard indicating an expected status and an actual status of each task.

UNITED STATES PATENT

Granted on December 29, 2009

Robert C. Anderson

Computer Aid, Inc.

US 7,640,225 B2

SYSTEM AND METHOD FOR PROCESS AUTOMATION AND ENFORCEMENT

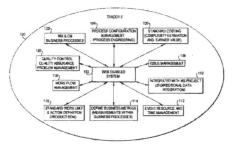

In process automation, processes are entered and enforced on team members through a Web interface. Processes are selected from a process library and can be updated as needed. Governance algorithms guide team members in carrying out the processes. The Web interface comprises a dashboard indicating an expected status and an actual status of each task.

The Director of Patents and Trademarks has received an application for a patent for a new and useful invention. The requirements of law have been complied with, and it has been determined that a patent on the invention shall be granted under the law. Therefore, this

United States Patent

Grants to the person or persons having title to this patent the right to exclude others from making, using or selling the invention throughout the United States of America for the term of the patent, subject to the payment of maintenance fees as provided by law.

David J. Kappos

Director of the United States Patent and Trademark Office

In 1998, I moved out of customer consulting and started working directly for Tony in research and development. In 2002, Tony wanted to expand the company internationally and wanted me to spend more and more time in Europe and Asia. After almost four-and-a-half years, hundreds of meetings, several dozen proposals submitted, we began to gain traction and win engagements. I had begun

Bob with clients at GE in Germany.

European operations while still managing the Process Development and Training Department, which had grown to thirteen employees. But then, as the international commitment grew, I gave its leadership to my successor, whom I'd had the pleasure of hiring and training.

The Andersons at Disneyworld, a trip that accompanied the CAI President's Award, 1999: Crystal, Bob as Indiana Jones, Vidya, and Colleen.

169

I am delighted to have contributed to Computer Aid's success. Today, CAI's global staff of 3,000 technical and managerial professionals serve hundreds of Fortune 100 and 500 companies, as well as government agencies around the world, with our unique IT process and metrics, methods, and tools that increase productivity, profitability, and competitiveness.

What more could you ask for? It's like a fairy tale.

Computerworld

I've worked for Computer Aid for almost a quarter century. I'm especially proud of my contribution to CAI's intellectual property—twelve process guides on application support services, ten training courses, fifteen brochures, twenty different sales presentations, a

a blog on IT service management that gets 1,400 hits per week, and, last but not least, Tracer Process and Data Management System —just to name a few.

Along the way, I was published in the December 2008 and the February 2007 issues of *Computerworld,* and my articles generated favorable responses from the magazine's readers worldwide. The 2007 article summarizes what I've learned about

Supporting Applications over a forty-year career in IT. It's titled "25 Time-Tested Truths About IT Support: Read 'Em and Reap Better Productivity, Service, and Overall Performance." It originated, by the way, from my professional experience, but also was influenced by insights that unfolded from my spiritual practices.

I've included it as Appendix C at the end of the book because it is generally applicable in many other professional settings and careers.

CHAPTER SEVENTEEN

Living the Journey

A master in the art of living draws no sharp distinction between
his work and his play, his labour and his leisure, his mind
and his body, his education and his recreation. He hardly
knows which is which. He simply pursues his vision of
excellence through whatever he is doing and leaves others
to determine whether he is working or playing. To himself
he always seems to be doing both. Enough for him that
he does it well. — Lawrence Pearsall Jacks, British educator
and Unitarian minister, in his book *Education Through
Recreation* (1932)

I've described Gururaj applying his thumbnail, or fork tines, or the
point of a steak knife to the center of my forehead in the precise
location of the inner eye of seeing and manifesting. The result
of that practice has become quite obvious in my work at CAI over
the years.

I'm reasonably bright, but what I've witnessed is that when you are
open to that universal source of energy, intelligence, and creativity
—and are not ego-focused—things come together naturally. This is
the essence of the creative process, at least for me. Respond to
intuition, share your intuition with other people, and watch the process
unfold. Like in one of those domino-tipping competitions you see on
TV every so often: when the first one is tipped, everything else just
falls into place.

Raspberry Jam on the End of My Nose

I never argue with results. I don't care how it happened. Gururaj could have put raspberry jam on the end of my nose for all I cared, if he had gotten the same results. I'm very, very fortunate that I had Gururaj, who basically said, "You are looking in the wrong direction," and he knew what practices would turn my attention in the right direction. He cared enough about me—warts and all—to see beyond my personality to that divine spark that is within us all, though initially I couldn't see it for myself.

I'd always had some access to the creative source, but mostly in latent form. When Gururaj saw my potential and figured out a technique to enhance my connection to the origin of all things, he based it on thousands of years of history in which the primordial teachings of Eastern wisdom have their roots.

Over time, my visions—let's call them—began to get clearer until today if something has to be done I don't think much about it; I allow a vision, or imagery, to take shape on its own. If I'm with a group of people, I'll be able to say a few words here and there and somehow they also will begin to see the vision and put their own gifts into that basic construct. Together we make something that is far better than any one of us alone could ever have done.

All I do is supply the outline and other creatively inspired people fill in the details. What comes out is something beautiful and we can all say, "Isn't that great! Look what we did!" I never fail to thank them for their contributions. That's how I've worked at Computer Aid for these many years. Everyone benefits from the sheer joy of watching something come from so-called "nothing." It's why I love my work.

Everything Intertwined

What causes this group dynamic? I don't altogether know. But I do know that there is wholeness to life. It's not spirituality over here, work over there, and relationships somewhere else. Everything is intertwined. Everything is a continuum, singular in its essence. We just have different focal points of attention at different times, but all of us share that common base of infinite intelligence, energy, and potential. It only needs to be actualized through the focused use of the resources we already have within us. Strengths get balanced, weaknesses get strengthened. Look within—it's all there.

My version of "looking within" is practicing the techniques of meditation taught to me by Gururaj and putting these principles into action in my life. Thus my outer life and inner life become inexorably intertwined. Not two, but one whole seamless existence expressing the same energy in different forms. *Outer* and *inner* are labels that are easily misunderstood—in reality there is only one whole from which different names, forms, and concepts come into being spontaneously and naturally. It is we who are out of balance, who divide the one into many and then set one against the other.

When I sit down, shut up, and close my eyes, all the nervousness and stray thoughts settle down. When I become quiet, that's when the creative thoughts express themselves more and begin to percolate into the level of the conscious mind from their unmanifest potential source. Then I can become a creative pathway from that silence to the outer world.

Watching Miracles Happen

My journey home is to find myself, "My True Self" (as Gururaj would say). In trying to find that inner source of my true self, my outer life seemed to fall into place more easily. Work wasn't just work—it was such a gas! I began to get a big kick out of going to work every day where I just kind of watched things get created—the dance of the inner and the outer—instead of swimming against the current of life, getting exhausted and frustrated.

In quiet moments during meditation, I got a chance to draw back and regroup in silence. And when I came out, I turned to work with a clear and focused mind. That creative part blossomed without having to do anything. I am fortunate that I learned to avoid the fatal mistake of thinking that creativity was mine. True creativity is impersonal and to personalize it is to limit it and block it from expressing itself in our lives. I watch creation like an amazed child.

All of us have creative potential, but so many of us are so busy struggling in the outer world that we think that we don't have time to go within. But if we do make the time to go within, meditate, or whatever you want to call it, we can draw on that incredible reservoir of energy, intelligence, and power that lies within each of us. We can manifest it in every aspect of our daily lives and watch the miracles happen. It's just amazing.

CHAPTER EIGHTEEN

Intuition Like a Sonar Ping

Life is simple, but it is so difficult to be simple.

— Gururaj Ananda Yogi

One of the most important things Gururaj taught is for us to love ourselves enough to trust our intuitions. You know those things that may not make sense to the mind, but feel right inside? Follow them. They are the Unknown, or the Real, trying to talk to us through the medium of inspiration. When we trust and listen to that voice, the more it can express itself through this body/mind into the world.

I'd like to describe how the intuitive creative process works for me. My technique is uniquely my own—every individual must find what works for them. The following is my personal experience of how intuitive awareness and the creative process have grown in my own life.

In business there's an old saying, "paralysis by analysis." That is where you keep analyzing a problem over and over and over but get no tangible results. What's happening is that a tremendous amount of mental, physical, and emotional energy is expended, but little gets done. What are we getting out of it but more analysis? It's just a self-perpetuating energy drain.

Many years ago, when I first became a programmer /analyst, I used to bother about problems that I couldn't figure out—how this system worked or where this bug was in a program. I'd mull it over, mull it over, and mull it over. I'd go nowhere and I'd be exhausted.

Over time, I learned to say, "Look. I'm going to drop it for now." But I'd put a pad of paper and a pencil by my bedside. In the middle of the night, I'd suddenly wake up and the answer would be there. I'd scribble it down. I'd go back to sleep, then I'd wake up and go to work with my pad and, sure enough, that was it. It worked perfectly.

I got the idea that when I needed an answer to a problem, the easiest way for me to get the answer was when I turned the problem into a question, a slight, almost effortless thought like a sonar ping, and then let it go. Have you heard of a sonar ping from a ship? A sound is broadcast and there is a return echo when it hits something. The process I'm trying to describe is something like that: Send out a question; then let go and allow the mind to become quiet and receptive with no anticipation, so that the echo, or the return answer, can more easily appear and be perceived. This was my first technique. I had to develop patience for the process to work without my interference.

A Bottomless Well at the Top of a Hill

The next phase in my intuitive process evolution was to create an internal image. When I had a problem in any area of my personal life or with work, anything I couldn't figure out that was bothering me, I would internally visualize a beautiful pastoral scene of a hill. I really got into it. The hill was covered with nice grass, and there were dandelions. Very pretty. Sunny day. Clouds and sky. At the top of the hill was a well. I could see the mortar and stones that made up the circular well and, of course, the wood that made up the top bar and the little bucket and rope that was attached to it.

Nobody was around…no buildings…no nothing. Just the well. I would walk to the top of the hill and think about what I needed, wanted, or what was bothering me. I'd speak it or drop it into the well, which had no bottom. It was infinite, simply blackness.

I would stand enjoying the day, doing absolutely nothing. After a period of time—sometimes very short, sometimes long—an echo would come back from the well. The answer would sound like a voice echoing from within the well and it was always the perfect answer for the question. I knew it was right because I tested it in my life. It always worked. It's a simple technique of visualization, asking, and then letting go of the outcome with an element of trust that the answer must exist and that it will come to you—basically one has to trust.

You see, moment by moment, microsecond by microsecond, the universe is changing. All the energies are shifting. Everything is in constant, dynamic motion. When you pose a question, the answer comes back spontaneously correct because nothing interferes with the convergent energies at that moment. And the clear and quiet mind perceives the answer.

When I would cast questions into the well, invariably everything would turn out perfectly. And I didn't do anything. I didn't mull it over and over, I didn't agonize over it, or get exhausted worrying about it. I didn't have to look at all the permutations. I began to trust the intuitive knowledge that comes from deep within, which is the source of every possible bit of knowledge in the universe. We cannot think our way to it, run our way to it, pray our way to it. As long as the mind is active, we are blocking that creative impulse that simply wants to appear and help us. There's nothing that we need do but ask and be silent. When we prepare ourselves and trust intuition, the more intuition flows in our life.

Embedded Answers

Now let's go to the next phase. When an issue would come up for me, just as the thought of it was created in the mind, the solution would correspondingly and instantaneously appear with it, without any effort.

I began to understand that within every single problem the answer is embedded within it.

You cannot have an issue or a problem without the answer being there simultaneously. We just have to figure out a way of listening for it or seeing it when it appears. You might think my "Tracer" software engineering would require a lot of thinking about complex subjects. Right? Nah! At that point, I would ping the universe and say, "I have to have a process for analyzing a support group and all the various functions and how they work together."

I would just sit in the office with my eyes closed or open. The inner screen of my mind would all of a sudden begin building things out of the silence. I could see it. This piece would be here; that piece would be there; and this is how they fit together. I would be watching but not thinking. The answers from deep within were just forming automatically by themselves.

I would write down some notes.

On some occasions, I'd get some of my colleagues together and I would share some of the ideas that built themselves within me. As I've described in developing the Tracer software, all of a sudden the creative processes of the whole group would kick into gear. The process had nothing to do with the group as individuals, but simply as an aggregate of energy expressing itself through different channels. It never seemed like hard *work*. We'd laugh and scribble ideas on blackboards…even tell jokes. All of a sudden, this incredible thing would emerge, and all of us knew automatically where we fit and what we were supposed to do. These energies would overlap and harmonize like a symphony or a wonderful chorus. We accomplished the work without saying, "We've got to hammer this out today, folks, this is gonna be really tough." The work just got done while we were all having fun.

Trust the Ping

The key is to stay out of our own way. What does that mean? It took me many years to trust intuition, trust that inner voice, the echo to my ping. I thought if I didn't control every piece of the process, I would fail. Something would screw up because I wasn't on top of it or in the middle of it micromanaging. Little by little, I learned to let go. Some people say, "Let go and let God." OK, it's a bit prosaic, but it is so absolutely true. I'm not saying that you don't have to do your homework. Gather the necessary resources, tools, information, and knowledge that form the framework of the house; then furnishing the house is easy. We simply have the impulse, or initial thought, about what's needed, then start doing. We stop the mind chatter and calm our fears, because fear and distrust stop creative intuition in its tracks.

That's what meditation and spiritual practice are about. It's allowing the mind to sink into the silence whose essence is not just peace but the source of all knowledge and creativity. Everything that has ever been or ever will be manifested is there in its potential form.

This reservoir of silent creativity is accessible to everyone regardless of the extremes and unpredictability of personality. For example, my own style is very intense yet I have found my way into this silence.

We are more than what we appear to be. We are not isolated individuals. We are a continuum. We are, at the most essential creative level, one singular force. We are in harmony, in touch with the entire creative force of the universe.

This knowing (not believing) comes from two things: First, by dipping into that creative potential through the meditation techniques that work for you. Second, by learning how to formulate the right question, then letting go of it with the intent of handing it off to the silent witness, whose nature is that creative force. After those two prerequisites, you simply wait without anxiety and without fear. As this intuitive creative process develops, you gain trust from the results. That gives you more confidence until you have absolute knowing that it will work every time.

The other essential piece of getting in touch with the creative flow is that it cannot simply be for personal ego gratification. If you're in it for that, then Pfffttttt! The water shuts off. If it is selfless—simply for the sake of doing no matter what that doing may be—then for the love of sharing and participating in this creative process called life, the universe will trip all over itself trying to get to you, to put all those things that are needed into place. It comes rushing. It may be through you, a five-year-old grandson, a relative, a colleague, a friend, a spouse, or a small voice within. When the unknown and unexpected manifests in our lives, it is that creative force in operation, and there is an internal recognition of rightness regardless of what shape it takes externally or internally.

We are co-creators with the Creator. We partake effortlessly in the creative process—only the scale is different, not the process. I haven't "worked" in the traditional sense of that word for I don't know how many years. I've turned to my job with a sense of excitement and enthusiasm to have fun with my friends and to create for the pure enjoyment of creating.

How do many people experience work? They box themselves into an egocentric package where the focus is on me and mine for money, power, and ego or sense gratification, thereby cutting off the creative process.

When there is true selflessness and no ego or sense of doership—no I, ME, MINE—you get the love of doing and watching others get that light in their eyes. That to me is the greatest thing in the world. There is no greater rush, no greater joy, which is why I love my work. It has taken me years to realize and trust intuition, to witness the unfolding in myself and in others.

Analytical and Intuitive Integration

I can explain the process a little further. The reason intuition works is that the analytical mind is disengaged in the intuitive process. There is a quiescent place where creative energy resides and intuits wholeness. The information appears without the linear process of analysis. Once it appears on the screen of mind, then the analytical mind can take action.

Everything in the universe is moving. If we don't trust ourselves and wait to act on something that presents to us, by the time we act, it's no longer the right answer because the energies have moved on. When an intuitive answer comes to us, we must get rid of fear and hesitation and act on it. It might not be perfect. Intuition doesn't fully blossom immediately. But as we progress, the intuitive process becomes fuller and answers come more quickly. You do course corrections as needed, and the answers begin to come more spontaneously. Each part of the brain functions in coordination and harmony with the others, effortlessly and instantaneously. As the process continues, the right answer for each new point in time manifests at the right time; because the energies are not static, the answers are not static.

I can explain the process in yet another way using the words of "Transactional Analysis," which provides a very good description of how the mental processes work. First of all, we have "Unconscious Incompetence." In other words, we're dumb and we don't even know it. Then we have "Conscious Incompetence," which means that we're dumb and we know it. Then there is "Conscious Competence," which means that we study and work very hard to learn our trade.

The final phase is "Unconscious Competence," where we simply do something repetitively so many times and study so hard in a certain area that we don't have to think much about it—we have worn a groove in the brain, and we more or less react out of engrained habit.

However, I would like to add one more dimension to this mental process. When we combine our engrained habit—"Unconscious Competence"—with meditation and spiritual practices, subtle internal energies are activated. This "subtle energy" is not part of brain function or the thinking process. It is a manifestation of Pure Awareness that uses the brain/mind as a conduit for spontaneous knowledge that existing circumstances shape into the appropriate thought and action.

Pure Awareness is the foundation of our existence. It spontaneously manifests what is needed in the moment without engaging the thinking analytical process. Because we are "Unconsciously Competent," we are not afraid that we don't know what we're doing, so we don't block that pure energy from manifesting what is needed in the HERE and NOW.

In this way, "Unconscious Competence" is augmented by spontaneous knowledge from deep within us, and that allows us to give shape and form to thought much more quickly with much less energy. These thoughts are more in tune with what is happening NOW. We are functioning in the realm of "Intuitive Competence," where right knowledge and right action flow spontaneously from us.

When we have incorporated that final level of intuition—"Intuitive Competence"—as a living reality within our daily lives, then whatever we do will be right for that moment. Regardless of what anybody else thinks, it will be completely in line with universal mind, universal purpose, or the will of God—I don't care how you refer to it.

No Bad Outcome

Things come and go. People come and go. The manifest world is created, stays for a while, then dissolves. Life can be uncomfortable when we hold on to things, are fearful, or operate from selfish motivation. We must trust that though something seems in the short term to be a failure or painful, it is there for a purpose. We can't just look at short-term profits and losses. When that part of the game is over, we look to all the paths that led to it and see that everything was necessary to happen as it did. There is no such thing as a bad outcome, but only a necessary outcome. Labeling it good or bad does not change what is!

Indelible intuitions transform our lives, take us to levels of greater realization, open the mind and heart, and become ours forever. In the scheme of things, it would be nice to have a new car or get the credit cards paid off. Sure. But when the true moments of clarity and profound peace come, they alter us in a subtle way forever. That's glorious and worthy of our praise. The universe knows what outcome is necessary to bring the correct balance to this life, this group, this planet. It is the source of its own creative impulse, of which we are a manifestation. Just trust it. That's all.

CHAPTER NINETEEN

Intuitive Writing

You have to leave the city of your comfort and go into the
wilderness of your intuition. You cannot get there by bus,
only by hard work, risking and by not quite knowing what
you are doing. What you will discover will be wonderful:
Yourself. — from the May 1980 *Connecticut College Commencement
Address* by Alan Alda, the actor who played Hawkeye in M*A*S*H, the
Emmy-winning television series set in the Korean War

I was never a good writer when I was young but, over time, I
gradually became reasonably proficient at business writing
throughout my career—proposals, budgets, analytical papers,
and system design specifications. My jobs have required it. But with
Gururaj's encouragement, I found that I could translate my spiritual
insights into essays and poetry. He encouraged me to begin writing
on any subject; but I could never sit down and just start writing.
Inspiration had to hit me so hard that I couldn't help putting words to
paper. Then the words would just materialize as if I were reading
from a book behind my eyes. Or, I would see a movie and simply write
about what I saw.

The writings that emerged came from that same intuitive creative
process that I take such pleasure in while I work with a business team
to accomplish a goal or to produce a process or product.

The intuitive writing started a few years after I met Gururaj. One
day while I was working at Armour Pharmaceutical back in 1983, I
was flipping through *Computerworld* magazine. My eyes fell on a

picture of thousands of little rabbits jumping around. All of a sudden, inspiration hit me for a poem. I was at work in my suit and tie and I started scribbling on a pad. The first five words came from Shakespeare, then the rest just flowed through the pen. I didn't change much of any wording after I finished. It came out word for word. I ripped the paper off the pad and later that evening I read "Dreamer" to Vidya and Gururaj, who at the time was staying with us at our home.

Dreamer

To sleep, perchance to dream of a thousand

worlds and a thousand faces.

Is the dream more real than the dreamer?

The dreamer, like a spider, spins the dream

in patterns beautiful from its own substance

and yet knows it not.

Remember, oh dreamer, that all dreams must

end with the coming of the dawn.

In the glow of dawn, silken threads of dreams

become illumined and transparent.

Arise, awake, oh dreamer of dreams.

The time of sleeping has passed.

Rise fully into knowledge and glory eternal.

The dream was your own creation in the sleep

of unknowing.

In the dawn of knowing, dreams

fade as shadows before the sun.

Arise, awake, oh dreamer of dreams, the time

of sleeping has passed.

When Gururaj first heard it, he was taken with it and wanted me to record him reading it. We must have done that at least fifteen or twenty times, with him using different dramatic inflections and gestures each time he read it. It was great fun, kind of like watching a professional actor reading Shakespeare. I'm not comparing my poem to Shakespeare, just Gururaj's dramatics. That was the impetus. As a result of that first poem, there were more times when an inspiration would hammer away inside of me, insistent to be written down.

One day I was meditating and all of a sudden a Technicolor 3-D movie of an eagle flying, complete with sound and music, began playing out in my head. The title of the movie was *Final Flight*. I sat watching this movie unfold on my interior screen; then when it ended, I was compelled to translate it into words. I started typing it on my computer as fast as I could, replaying as much as I could remember. A little short story emerged.

Final Flight

High upon the craggy mountainside the great eagle unfurls his

golden wings and launches into the early morning azure sky for

one final flight.

Though spiraling to ever greater heights, hardly a flicker of
feather can be seen, for it is not by wing and feather alone is
he borne aloft but by the soft breath of sky father
warmed by the light of the great golden disk which shines above.

He has learned the secret of flight.

Higher and higher he soars until the earth itself appears but a
hazy field of merging colors far below. He looks one last time
to the earth and voices a single cry as if to say farewell to the
creatures who have been his companions over these
many seasons.

Some hear his call and look skyward with a smile for they know
their brother is going home. Others look about curiously wondering
from where this soulful cry has come. Soon all return to their
daily tasks forgetting the small speck receding in morning's light.

Upward ever upward he soars, gliding silently, effortlessly on
huge golden wings through the endless canopy of blue.

No longer does he look earthward, for now his eyes are fixed
steadily on the great golden disk of light shining brilliantly

above him. Its brilliance no longer hurts his eyes as it did in the beginning of his seeing, for over the seasons, little by little, he has accustomed his eyes to its light.

He has grown to love the great golden disk of light even more than life itself, for to him it was pure beauty giving unceasingly of its warmth and light to all, asking nothing in return.

The more he looked at its beautiful golden light, the more his love grew. It seemed to beckon him, whispering in his heart, "Come to me, my beloved. You have flown high and given unselfishly of your beauty to the world. Now it is time to come home."

Onward he soars, with solitude his only companion. At times his powerful body feels heavy and his goal seems far away but he does not falter, for the golden disk of light is forever beckoning.

Though his resolve is steadfast, Earth Mother does not give up her children easily. She pulls at every fiber of his being, calling for him to give up this fruitless quest and return to her world and a life where all love and admire him.

His body once sleek and strong is now racked with pain, and flight becomes unbearable. He cries out in despair, for he knows that in only a few moments his strength will fail and he will plummet downward to be crushed and broken…never to fly again, never to reach his great golden disk shining so beautifully just out of reach.

In those final moments when all seems lost, a great calm descends upon him, and strength such as he has never known floods his being, a strength that came not from his body but from the light of the golden disk. The light gently envelopes him and lifts him beyond fear and pain.

The quiet voice speaks one final time within his heart, saying, "Welcome home, beloved."

The golden light and his body seem to shimmer, becoming infused with each other. It is now hard to tell where his body ends and the golden light begins.

In a final burst of joy, golden light merges with golden feather, becoming one.

Now only the great golden disk of light remains awaiting the next final flight....

It was never, "Sit down and think about writing." If inspiration kicked me in the ass and wouldn't leave me alone until I wrote the words down, only then I would write. Only after I wrote it down could I feel at peace. Like a stick jabbing at my butt: Write it down now! I had to write it down or otherwise I would be miserable. Most of my writings were like that—violent inspiration took hold and made demands.

"The Companion" also emerged when I was meditating. Gururaj and I were disembodied entities moving through space and time through a field of stars, going momentarily from one planet to another like way stations, embodying, then leaving, then moving on together again. From that vision, I wrote this poem.

The Companion

Down the endless corridor of time, my companion

and I have traveled. Many doors have we opened

sublime glories to behold.

Why travel we together? It is love which binds us,

the two becoming one. It is love of love which

separates us, appearing as two.

My beloved, myself, come let us walk hand in hand

through timeless time enjoying the joy of shared love.

The ecstasy of creation's sway is the path upon which we

tread, tarrying from time to time, fragrant flowers to gather

and then move on.

As the cloak of eternal silence enfolds us, echoes of

laughter pulse through the starry night bringing sparkles

of delight.

Another journey ended, another journey begun . . .

I'm not a writer or a poet by nature. The writings I've shared in this chapter and those I've included in Appendix D of this book are the only creative writing I've ever done, but in some ways I guess they represent an important aspect of my spiritual journey. I've had no inspiration to write more poetry in recent years. When they happened, they happened. I could not and cannot force it. But for a time, when something demanded to be written out, I was not left in peace until I got it out. Other inspirations passed through, but I couldn't hold on to them and they were never written. I just endured the jabbing because they were gone before paper or computer was close at hand.

Warrior's Song: The Journey Home, though prose and not poetry, is one of those butt jabbings. Over the course of at least thirty years, first Gururaj then many other people told me to write a book. I put it off and put it off as long as I could, until the butt jabbing became simply unbearable! You are reading the result. Initially I "spoke" the first draft intuitively. Then, more than fourteen hours of recordings were transcribed. Subsequently, several written drafts were required to refine the narrative into something readable. Now I feel a measure of peace from the considerable butt jabbing I have been getting for so many years.

CHAPTER TWENTY

Traveler's Tapestry

I soon realized that no journey carries one far unless, as it extends into the world around us, it goes an equal distance into the world within. — Attributed to Lillian Smith (1897-1966), American southern writer and social activist

T he grown man, who as a young boy searched for a spaceship ride home in the dry river washes of the Nevada desert, learned from Gururaj that home is not a place or a time. Home is inside of you. If you are grounded in your true Self, anywhere your footsteps fall is home. Any place your eyes see is home. All people, not just your biological relatives, are your brothers and sisters. All religions, your religion. All faiths, your faith.

My travels, both domestic and international, have contributed to a rich storehouse of cultural appreciation and have reinforced my gradually maturing spiritual philosophy of the basic unity of all humanity.

The love we feel toward our family—why can't we feel it for the larger family of human kind? Can we be flexible enough to carry no fixed judgments? Want more opening of the heart? We can break down the walls that shut us off from the wider world of possibilities. If we take chances, which are scary on many occasions, the rewards far outweigh the risks.

Maha Kumbh Mela

In January 2001, at the change of the millennium, I went to India to attend the Maha Kumbh Mela, a great Hindu religious fair held every 144 years.

I didn't want to miss this one! Though I wasn't a Hindu, it was a once-in-a-lifetime, unique event that I knew could hold some new understandings for me.

For the Maha Kumbh Mela, some of the holy men and mystics come down out of the Himalayas only once in a lifetime into the flood plains of the Ganges River to participate in this great religious festival.

The group I went with was called the Himalayan Institute (from Pennsylvania) and I stayed at their ashram (a bunch of tents in the middle of the jungle), which was just two kilometers down the banks of the Ganges from the festival site at Allahabad.

I'd never been to India before. I was listening to chanting twenty-four hours a day in an ancient culture that's more than 3,500 years old. The Indian people, though generally very poor in money, are very rich in spirit. Gentle people. Kind people. They never yelled or swore to each other in traffic, though it was some of the most horrific I've ever seen. The people had a sense of goodness about them.

I bartered for everything—not that they were just trying to get the best price out of me, but that's how they got to know people. Bartering was a social custom. I got pretty good at it—even bargaining for the price of a carrot. You'd have a leisurely cup of tea and barter over an item. It was great fun.

I toured ancient temples. I saw where Buddha gave his first sermon. I saw a branch of the Bodhi tree he was sitting under when he received enlightenment. I brought Vidya three leaves from the Bodhi tree. I brought water back from the Ganges River, though sadly it leaked out somewhere along the journey home. I brought back beautiful scarves for friends.

The trip was a personal milestone. And in its way prepared me to take on new responsibilities in CAI international expansion.

The World as My Home

In 2002, Tony wanted to expand the business globally. He asked me to start by acquiring a toehold in the UK. That meant I lived and worked in the UK and all over Europe and Asia two weeks out of four, for four-and-a-half years.

CAI maintained a house in Beaconsfield, northwest of London, near Slough, and an office in downtown London. We travelled from London to Wales and Scotland, from east to west coasts. I became well acquainted with the people and the history of the UK.

Using England as our base, we travelled all over Europe, sometimes two or three trips in one week in search of new business: Sweden, Ireland, Romania, France, the Netherlands, and Germany. I had to get two or three sets of inserts for the stamps in my passport. I was constantly in an airport or on an airplane going somewhere.

Then we sought business in Tokyo, Japan; Istanbul, Turkey; Shanghai, China; Sydney, Australia; and Hanoi, Vietnam. In a prior time of life it would not have been a good thing to be in Hanoi, but the second time around it was a wonderful trip. I travelled to Saigon (Ho Chi Minh City), then on to Singapore in Malaysia, and Manila in the Philippines.

I've learned to become a chameleon, honest and genuine, but a chameleon. Wherever I am, I adopt local customs and conditions. I wear different uniforms for each different role, but I am the same actor. I've learned simply to fit into and work creatively in business and social settings in any culture.

I travelled to Majorca as a young man learning TM. Following Gururaj, I went to Spain, Cyprus, and England. Then CAI business extended my travel around the world. I've bounced around from one end of this planet to the other. More or less, the whole world is my home, including the ocean depths.

Diving into the Beauty of the Deep

A very dear friend, Russell Amaru, with whom I grew up from fourteen years old at Las Vegas High, encouraged me to learn to scuba dive.

"Bob, you've just got to go to get your certification," he said. "That's the only way to enjoy the depths and beauty of the ocean, which is another world entirely."

My sister, Jody, gave me five free days in Bermuda. Russ and I used the gift to get to a great dive site where I could also take my dive training.

What I didn't know at first is that it takes three to four weeks to get certified in open water diving. There's a 250-page book to almost memorize, seven tests including a long final exam, seven videos (more than five hours), swimming pool exercises, then four open water dives on top of that. I decided to hire a private instructor. I got certified from ground zero, not missing any of the steps, in two-and-a-half days! I memorized the book overnight.

I had Russ quizzing me for the tests. I had helped him study geology in college, so I figured turn about was fair play. I went through the full course, skipping nothing, and by the beginning of the second day I was in the pool. I really took to it. On the morning of the third day I did my four certification dives all in one day, though typically you only do a couple of dives a day. I could do four in a day because we were in shallow water, at thirty or forty feet.

Of course I got my own tanks, wet suits, and regulators, and, in time, I went for advanced certifications. That meant I could do deeper dives and navigate underwater.

My first real diving trip was at the island of Cozumel, on the eastern coast of Mexico's Yucatan Peninsula where reef varieties are numerous in the offshore waters. The bottom of the ocean floor looked like a big pile of powdered sugar. I was gliding above an alien seascape like a visitor from another planet.

After missing some absolutely stunning photo opportunities, I decided to buy a really good underwater camera. In my own mind, I looked like Jacque Cousteau, but most likely I favored a Martian on steroids. When doing underwater photography I paid more attention to the beautiful surroundings and I was always looking for the next great shot.

But no photograph can do justice to the beauty of those coral reefs, the fish, the turtles, the lobsters, and the rays. On one particularly exciting dive, I chased down an eagle ray with a ten-foot span and got a great shot, even though I used most of my air swimming like a mad man to get it. You have to know what you are doing and stay oriented at all times. You never get too near the coral

because it's a fragile ecosystem. On some dives, there's a little edginess to the experience—when you're right on the continental shelf where the drop is 3,000 feet straight down. You have to gauge your descents and ascents slowly and carefully lest you get the bends or worse—RUN OUT OF AIR! And, it's essential to know all of your equipment, not just your camera.

Cozumel is my favorite diving spot. I've taken my daughters there, and they also have been certified.

It's All Holy Land

In the summer of 2011, my spiritual brother, Lee Swanson, and I took a spontaneous five-day trip to the Holy Land in the Middle East. We road camels and visited the Garden of Gethsemane, the site of the Last Supper, and the Holy Sepulchre where Jesus' body was buried. I touched the rock where Jesus was dressed in his burial robe. And we visited Golgotha where Jesus was crucified, and the tomb of Mary, the mother of Jesus. During our trip we visited Masada, overlooking the Dead Sea, where 900 Jews—men, women, and children— were besieged by a Roman legion and committed suicide rather than be captured.

If you were to draw colorful lines on the routes of every plane trip I've taken, the globe would look like a beautiful tapestry. And I continue to travel for work and for pleasure. On the following pages I've included a collection of my travel photos, by country, beginning in the London.

**TOP: Big Ben and the Houses of Parliament across the Thames.
BOTTOM: Bob as Holmes with daughter Crystal as Watson at the Sherlock
Holmes Museum, 221b Baker Street, London.**

RIGHT: Nelson's Column in the middle of Trafalgar Square, London.

BELOW: Armor exhibit at Tower of London.

LEFT: Royal Guard at Tower of London.

BELOW: Armored horse (and rider) at Tower of London.

ABOVE: Stonehenge, a prehistoric stone monument near Bath, England.

BELOW: The tomb, in St. Paul's Cathedral, of British Admiral Horatio Nelson (one of Bob's heroes) who won the Battle of Trafalgar (one of the greatest naval victories in history).

STOCKHOLM, SWEDEN

LEFT: Between business meetings, Bob takes a a break by one of the interesting scuptural fountains in the Town Square.

BELOW: Bob in front of a city harbour panorama with a Viking longboat moored in the distance.

PARIS, FRANCE

ABOVE: The Eiffel Tower.

BELOW: Notre Dame Cathedral.

ABOVE: Arc de Triomphe at night.

BELOW: Arc de Triomphe in middle of a busy day.

ISTANBUL, TURKEY

ABOVE: Blue Mosque.
BELOW: Whirling Dervish in classical dress.

ABOVE: Classic belly dancer.

BELOW: Traditional Turkish Dancer.

VIETNAM

ABOVE: Restaurant musical entertainer and Bob in Hanoi.

LEFT: Model ship built in Saigon that now sits in Bob's office in Harrisburg, Pennsylvania.

SINGAPORE

Bob with his friend the snake.

CARIBBEAN

Bob with the birds of St. Martin Island.

JAPAN

ABOVE: Buddhist Temple, Kyoto.

LEFT: Bonsai tree in hotel garden, Tokyo.

Buddhist Temple near Tokyo.

Waterfall in the gardens at the New Otani Hotel, Tokyo.

Buddhist Temple, Kyoto.

213

SHANGHAI, CHINA

ABOVE: Traditional architecture in shopping district, Shanghai.

BELOW: Nightlife in Shanghai.

INDIA

LEFT: Durga Hindu Temple in Benares, India.

ABOVE: Palaces that the monkeys took over from the regal Maharajas, along the Ganges River in Benares, India.

LEFT: Bob inside the temple where Buddha gave his first talk.

BELOW: Temple built where Buddha gave his first talk, Sarnath, India.

Bob on the Ganges River near the site of the Maha Kumbh Mela festival, held near Allahabad only once every 144 years.

SYDNEY, AUSTRALIA

Bob at Sydney Harbour with the world famous Sydney Opera House in the background.

217

ABOVE: "Git along little dogies!"

BELOW: Bob and his "mate" inside the
Natural Science Museum at Darling Harbour.

Outside the Natural Science Museum at Darling Harbour.

ABOVE: Beautiful butterfly collection inside the Natural Science Museum.

BELOW: Bob and a resting Kangaroo at the Natural Science Museum.

ABOVE: Bob with a sleepy Koala bear (a native to Australia) at the Sydney Zoo.

BELOW: Another sleepy Koala.

COZYMEL, MEXICO

TOP LEFT:
Bob on a dive boat.

TOP RIGHT: Bob on
the beach ready for
snorkeling.

BOTTOM:
Big Turtle that Bob
photographed above
the powdered
sugar sand on the
ocean floor.

TOP and BOTTOM: Two kinds of beautiful and fragile coral.

223

ABOVE: Bob and daughter Crystal floating above the powered sugar sand on the ocean floor.

BELOW: Diving buddies—Bob's daughters, Crystal and Colleen.

THE HOLY LAND

ABOVE: 2,000-year-old olive trees inside the Garden of Gethsemane where Jesus went with his disciples to pray after the Last Supper.

BELOW: Bob at the site of the Last Supper.

ABOVE: Brother Lee Swanson and Bob at the Church of the Holy Sepulchre in Jerusalem (where Jesus was buried).

BELOW: Brother Lee and Bob at Masada where 900 Jews committed suicide rather than surrender to the Romans.

ABOVE: Brother Lee on the camel, with Bob standing beside him, near Garden of Gethsemane.

BELOW: They switched.

227

ABOVE: Lee and Bob at the tomb of Mary the Mother of Jesus in the old city of Jerusalem.

BELOW: Bob in front of the Muslim Dome of Rock, a holy site in the old city of Jerusalem.

CHAPTER TWENTY-ONE

Never Argue with What Is
—Is Always Wins

On the journey of the warrior-bodhisattva, the path goes down, not up, as if the mountain pointed toward the earth instead of the sky. Instead of transcending the suffering of all creatures, we move toward the turbulence and doubt however we can. We explore the reality and unpredictability of insecurity and pain, and we try not to push it away. If it takes years, if it takes lifetimes, we let it be as it is. At our own pace, without speed or aggression, we move down and down and down. With us move millions of others, companions in awakening from fear. — Pema Chödrön, American Buddhist Nun in the Tibetan Tradition, in her book *Comfortable with Uncertainty* (2002)

I n the first fifty-five years of my life I was bulletproof. With the exception of my adolescent bout of mono and a touch of asthma, I didn't get so much as a head cold. I could and did put myself into and through circumstances and situations that would have killed most people. I could do some of the most absurdly dangerous things and nothing would break.

I survived combat in Vietnam without so much as a scratch, really. It was as if a protective shield was around me. If people have guardian angels, I had a full platoon and a heavy weapons squad that lived on

Maalox and Tums. They had a full-time job since I had a habit of seeking out danger and seeing how close to the edge I could go and not fall off. When I think of some of the things I did, particularly in combat, I shake my head and say to myself, "You sure were a dumb shit."

In January 2001, after I went to India to attend the Maha Kumbh Mela, the physically challenging part of my life began. On the way back home from India, on a train, I got a spider bite. That was the beginning of another cycle of learning in life, another battlefield.

Although my spiritual framework was thriving, it was time for me to learn a deeper lesson: How can you understand and empathize with other people's suffering unless you have experienced similar pain yourself?

By the time I got back to the United States, my hand had turned black, and blood poisoning had set in. I was treated with antibiotics, but I contracted a usually fatal arterial disease—an autoimmune response to the spider venom or the heavy dose of antibiotics that I got in the hospital—that hit my kidneys. I endured chemotherapy for nine months, still working full time. The first half of every day was rough—I was horribly sick from the chemotherapy. My kidneys were functioning at only 70 percent. After about two years, my blood levels stabilized and round one of my physical challenges subsided. My daughter Colleen, who is a nurse, has told me that less than 50 percent of people survive five years after the onset of this disease. I'm glad I didn't know that initially.

In 2004, I injured my back simply lifting a couch. As a result of tests, I found out I had a very aggressive degenerative spinal disorder that eats away at the vertebrae and disks. Thereafter, I endured twenty invasive procedures over three years to stem the chronic pain caused by the degeneration. In 2007, 2009, and 2012, three major surgeries were required to correct damage as the disease progressed up the spine.

230

The first operation to remove two discs in June 2007 failed because my body rejected the bone from the bone bank (cadaver bone). A fracture was forming, and the pain was unbearable. A second surgery in February 2010 was performed by a different neurosurgeon, a brilliant young man in his forties named Dr. Devanand Dominique. He used my own bone, carved out of bone spurs that were growing into the nerve channels, and fused my spine again, pinning it on both sides. I also had eight three-inch screws (each a quarter-inch in diameter), two rods (four inches long), and a titanium cage placed around the new bone graphs. Oddly enough, and comforting at the same time, both Dr. Dominique's mother and daughter were named Vidya (same as my wife's spiritual name).

The pain continued, but was manageable with heavy-duty pain medication. When the pain worsened again—my legs would actually fold up and I would fall to the ground in agonizing pain—the doctor told me I just had the bad luck of the disease progressing up to the next level of the spine. Two vertebrae were periodically pinching off a main nerve to my legs.

I had a third surgery in June 2012. In this one, more screws were put in, and more bars and another cage were placed around the spine. Dr. Dominique took out the seven screws from the previous surgery. So, in the space of about twenty months, Dr. Dominique and I had spent more than seventeen hours in an operating room where I was carved up like a side of beef.

The jury is still out on the overall effectiveness of the most recent surgery. While I was recuperating, I found I had a problem with the tendons in my hand and another surgery was looming. Fortunately, there is a procedure that could cure that problem (a very painful injection), and I had that done a few weeks after the spinal surgery.

As Mother Theresa said, "*I know God won't give me anything I can't handle.*" But let me tell you, I am reaching that point of enough is enough. I am not sure how much I've learned from the past ten years of physical trauma, but I sure hope I have passed the course. I still work full time, even though some mornings the pain is so severe that I have to crawl out of bed.

You play the cards that you are dealt the best way you can. So why bitch and moan about circumstances? Do what you can, then let it go. After all, there is nothing more you can do, so why add insult to injury by developing a bad attitude? Just put one foot in front of the other and keep going. It could be worse!

Agent Orange and PTSD

Continuing my lessons in compassion and courage, simultaneous with the onset of back pain several years ago, I began to experience symptoms of Post Traumatic Stress Disorder (PTSD) as the result of combat in Vietnam forty years earlier. How could that be, so long after my war experience? It was explained to me that PTSD is like a time bomb waiting for the right combination of circumstances to set it off. I've found out a lot about suffering—mine and that of many other war veterans—through my own process of recovery.

I have been given information that also indicates there is a high probability my spinal degeneration was caused by prolonged exposure to the chemical defoliant Agent Orange, which was sprayed very heavily in the areas where I lived and fought for two years in Vietnam. The chemical dioxin is one of the worse carcinogens (cancer-causing agents) in the world today.

I, along with many of my fellow Marines who flew combat missions in that poisonous battleground, have been classified by the Veterans Administration as 100 percent permanently and completely disabled. When I get a house dropped on my head, I don't mess around—it's not a small house, but a mansion!

A Real Warrior Asks for Help

I am still working full time, and though I'm not supposed to lift anything heavier than a phonebook, I push the limits of my body, mind, and spirit every day. I have had physical limitations piled high and deep, but I simply keep putting one foot in front of the other, and get help from the VA and others as much as I can. A real warrior has the courage to ask for help when the load gets too heavy, so he can live to fight another day.

I can honestly say I would never have made it through more than a decade of physical and emotional pain without my meditation practice and the teachings I received from Gururaj. They were engrained as an integral part of my body, mind, and spirit, operating every day through the constant bombardment from all directions of the compass. In this context, my spiritual path has saved my physical ass.

I would like to share some thoughts from a fellow warrior who also suffers from PTSD. His essay, "No Peace," reflects some of the stress we endured when we came back to the States after our tours in combat in Vietnam.

No Peace
We came home nearly forty years ago to a place that we didn't know, and that didn't know us. We tried our best to fit in, to go back in time, trying to return to who we were and what we had been just a few short years earlier. For most of us it didn't work. The world that we knew, and thought they knew us, was no longer there, gone, along with our innocence, and a lot of our friends. Many things, and in some cases, people, that just a few years earlier had meant so much to us, meant nothing now, and the feeling was mutual. Often, the one that had promised to wait forever didn't, but we never knew it until we came home. Sometimes, even the churches

233

that we went to before didn't want us sitting in the same pews with "good" people on Sunday. After all. . .WE had blood on our hands. Things like this are hard to forget, or forgive.

Our "before Nam" buddies, the ones who didn't go, weren't anymore. The ones that would still talk to us just wanted to know what we had "DONE" over there. And then didn't want to listen when we told them. They soon figured out that we weren't putting up with their bullshit, and stopped coming around. We had lost friends before. . .We tried to forget. . . .

So, time goes by, many of us found someone who accepted us, and was willing to put up with our little "quirks." Soon we had kids, a place to live, and in some instances, after many failed attempts, a pretty decent job. And, we had a dog (him we could trust). It seemed as if we had everything we needed. . . .We almost forgot. . . BUT . . .

But there was NO PEACE. There was NEVER any PEACE. Not really. Things were just never the same for us. Everyone always wondered why but didn't really want to know. Some people said, "If it's that Vietnam thing, get over it. It wasn't really a war, and besides it was a long time ago. Grow up." Most people don't deserve to know, most never will. We do.

The people we choose to let into our lives are either like us, or accept us for who we are. We seem to surround ourselves with others who like us, cannot forget, yet who we know we can forever, and always, really trust. They know what we are about, what is in our hearts, and that share the love we have for each other. WE WILL NEVER FORGET, That's what makes us. . .The Vietnam Veteran. . . BROTHERS FOREVER.

Jim Fox, 1st Cav, 1967-68
March 22, 2012, Veteran's Common Bond Blog
Published in *Warrior's Song: The Journey Home* with permission from thuysmithinternationaloutreach.org/ whose mission is to promote kindness, compassion, and healing in the world

Bob in his dress blues at the 2013 Vietnam Veterans Memorial Day Parade, Washington D.C.

CHAPTER TWENTY-TWO

Warrior's Song

There is no such thing as an ex-Marine.... There is no better testament to the solid foundation we imbue than the countless number of Marines no longer on active duty who credit their successes to the skills and lessons learned in the Corps. — from the official Marine Corps website at http://www.marines.com/history-heritage

Honor, Courage, Commitment. Picture a teenager on the cusp of manhood hanging from the door of a helicopter by one leg and no belt in desperate pursuit of his balance amid the fire of combat. Now picture him in a tent reading philosophy by the light of a single candle.

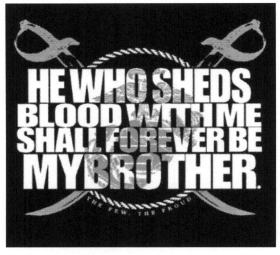

The core values awakened in me as a Marine in my youth have never left me. They were forged in harm's way, side by side with brothers who were singing the same song. When things were bad and the world was going up in flames around us, we were all sustained by these core values, which were forged by our training into our very souls and are the essence of the warrior spirit. These values have

The Three Servicemen bronze statue at the Vietnam War Memorial, Washington, D.C.

sustained Marines through countless battles on many shores and climes, in many times. These values are the foundation, the bedrock, of the greatest warriors the world has ever known: the United States Marine Corps.

Marine Corps values are the melodic line of my life around which everything else is arranged—especially my spiritual pursuits.

Character determines the course of your life.

Marines are honest. Marines are courageous in the face of adversity. They innovate, adapt, and overcome, even when their decisions or actions will not win any popularity contests. They stand by their decisions and actions, taking full responsibility, making no excuses. Marines are committed to the best that's in them. They do their best to

237

live up to the highest standards, and that's what distinguishes the United States Marine from all other warriors.

As a Marine and a civilian, I've made many mistakes, but I've tried to learn from those mistakes. That goes hand-in-hand with the core values. It's called strength of character. If somebody in your life isn't making mistakes, he or she is static, not doing anything. It does not matter how many times you fall. What is really important is that you pick yourself up and learn a little more each time you stumble.

Marines never break the faith. They would sooner die than let down a brother Marine or the Corps. That is honor. That is one of the cornerstones of my life. I live and die by my word.

When Marines are in combat, we always look out for our brother Marines first, ourselves second. We are a brotherhood, a family. We have each other's backs.

Marine relationships become more intense, even more priceless, than relationships in civilian life—brother and sister, mother and son, husband and wife. In these family relationships, in most cases you see only what the other person wants you to see. By contrast, the Marine bond is forged in a fire that welds you together in the crucible of combat. I'm not overstating that. You cannot hide anything when you are on the knife's edge between life and death.

This is when TRUE character is revealed. Marines know that honor is more important than life itself. Material things come and go. But nobody can take away your honor or your character. You can give them away, but no one can take them. When you die, everything else gets left behind, but your character? You take it with you. If you were a jerk thinking only of yourself, how much you could grab, how you could step on people and succeed on the backs of others through lying and manipulation—what is that going to say at the summation of your life? You did nothing and you take nothing with you. But a man of honor succeeds through hard work and pulling others along when he can and literally running out into the battlefield and dragging them out of danger. You take core values with you to the bank of the eternal. They are the coin of the realm when the body is no more.

In any branch of military service, when you are in a situation where you live or die based on the person next to you, that becomes an incredibly intense heat that welds the metal of two into one. Combat reduces everything down to the most basic dichotomy: life or death. You've heard about Marines who jump on hand grenades to save brother Marines? You don't think. You act. They are your brothers. Their lives come before your life spontaneously, without thought.

Seems to me that in the rest of our relationships there are no life/death issues. Therefore, it takes longer in civilian life to develop that kind of trust and respect. Nevertheless, Marine combat experience engrained in me a sense of being honorable and reliable, being loyal and committed, that I've carried into civilian life—whether I'm relating to a friend or family member, or to my wife and children, or to my employer. Core values impact every aspect of my life.

The kind of trust I'm talking about has to build over time. You build it in combat when you are fighting back to back, even saving each other's lives. In civilian life, it's not that easy. People say one thing and mean another. They have hidden agendas. You must have a close relationship for an extended time to create the kind of mutual trust and commitment a Marine expects in relationship.

Take my boss, Tony Salvaggio, and another friend and colleague, Mike Kucek, at Computer Aid. We'll soon celebrate twenty-five years together—a good portion of a lifetime. In that time, you really get to know someone in the heat of a different kind of battle. The battles of the business world can be as intense as those where bullets are flying around. Yes, just as I would for my Marine brothers, I would do anything for them because I know they would never break the faith with me. That doesn't mean I would do foolish things, or that I don't disagree with them when I believe they are about to make a mistake. Some of our discussions can get pretty intense, but always respectful.

Once people join your close sphere of comrades, once they pass muster, they are there for life.

Tony, Mike, Lee, Russell, and a very few others are like members of my Marine Corps family for the rest of my life. I'd take a bullet for any one of them in a heartbeat.

In addition to my Marine brothers and extended family of friends, I'm blessed with blood family who are the world's best: My wife, Vidya; our two daughters, Colleen and Crystal, both of their husbands and my dear grandchildren; my sister, Jody; my brother, Donald Anderson; and above all, my Mom. My immediate family gives me a sense of joy and belonging that makes getting up in the morning worth the effort.

ABOVE: Brothers in arms VMO-2 squadron at a reunion in Kittyhawk, NC.

BELOW LEFT: Bob on model of Wright Brothers' plane, Kitty Hawk
BELOW RIGHT: Echo Company Marine Corps Birthday Ball, Harrisburg, PA

Vidya and Bob at the Marine Corps Birthday Ball in Harrisburg.

Whether as a Marine or as a civilian, when it's time to gear up and go into battle, you just go do it.

No second thoughts.

You don't have to question who stands with you, who watches your back, or who you trust with your life—you already know: family and a small circle of close friends who have proven themselves on life's battlefield.

And then there's Gururaj. This is a special case where my commitment is not just to a physical form, but to an even greater power of love and compassion that he embodied and lived. That kind of commitment goes beyond words or even life and death.

Reunion of Brothers

When I reunite with my group of fellow squadron mates from VMO-2, it's like a bunch of more-than-brothers gathered. You reminisce, you laugh, you tell jokes about each other; and below the surface, there is a strong and relentless current that binds you together. No words can express it, but it is keenly felt and never fades. Terry Bowman was the crew chief in the dangling belt escapade I described in CHAPTER TWO when I successfully unjammed a gun and narrowly escaped death. I have a special relationship with him. Until a reunion last year, we didn't even know that he lives in Hagerstown, Pennsylvania, only an hour from my house in Boiling Springs. It was at the same gathering when we put two and two together to realize we shared the same incident.

I'll never forget Terry screaming, "Get the fuck in here, you moron!" as I dangled outside the helicopter within seconds of annihilation.

After that, Vidya and I were attending a Pop-a-Smoke USMC Combat Helicopter Association reunion in Dallas, Texas. We were headed to the VMO-2 Squadron Operations hut. A guy I didn't recognize came out of the bar as we were approaching.

He said, "Are you Bob Anderson?"

I said "Yes."

"Then you must be the guy who was dangling outside the Huey in a hot zone!" Vidya was standing right next to me and can vouch for this encounter.

"Yeah, that was me."

I was truly delighted that my crazy stunt had become part of squadron folklore. Mine was fairly simple compared to many of these guys' stories, though. Some of them had helicopters blown out from beneath them. One example is Terry Bowman's helicopter, which looked like a piece of crumpled paper when it crashed.

Terry (who was the crew chief), the helicopter's pilot, and the gunner escaped, but the co-pilot, Jerry Ringenberg, died when the Huey crashed—he had the control stick jammed into his head.

Combat after-action report and Air Medal Citation for completing combat missions where fired upon and fire was returned.

As amazing as those reunions were, there was yet another meeting so improbable that I still have a hard time believing it actually happened. While in Vancouver, British Columbia, attending a Gururaj meditation course, I was having a Bloody Mary in the bar to get rid of a hangover. I was just in a shirt and Levis, no Marine markings of any kind (except for the Eagle, Globe, and Anchor tattoo on my upper left arm).

This guy came up to me. For some reason I guess I looked familiar to him. As we talked, the connection emerged, and I was dumbfounded, as was he.

"Were you a Marine in Vietnam?

I said, "Yes, I was a door gunner in Huey Gunships of VMO-2."

"Did you ever do 'med evac'?" I said, "Rarely, because we were gunships, but on special occasions, certainly."

"Do you remember pulling a wounded Marine into the helicopter, then flying him to Charlie Med?"

I remembered flying a wounded Marine into Charlie Med only once. So, I said yes. In combat, our squadron would periodically go on a "dust-off" (med evac) mission and take wounded out of the zone.

Normally this was done in a "slick" (no guns). It was tight quarters in a gunship helicopter, but we always had room for somebody wounded. As I remember (forty years after the fact), we were called in to support some Marine ground elements with our guns. After hosing down the area, we were asked if we could take out one casualty. This guy was hurt pretty bad when I helped pull him in. We took off fast, before we got our butts blown off. We flew him to a hospital area called Charlie Med not far from Da Nang.

I would never have believed it. Sitting in a bar in Vancouver, that same fellow was the guy I pulled into the helicopter!

"Thank you for saving my life," he said.

Bizarre. Surreal. We talked for hours. It's the kind of thing that sends a shiver up your spine, and almost brings tears to your eyes—love deeper than anything that you can label as love. I don't know what to call it. But as a Marine, it gets impressed indelibly into your soul, and you carry it with you your entire life. You honor your fellow Marines throughout your life no matter your vocation or where you go.

Picture the man I've become, collaborating in a boardroom or meditating in my chair at home, wrapped in a warm blanket. Wherever I am, the values hold: Honor. Courage. Commitment.

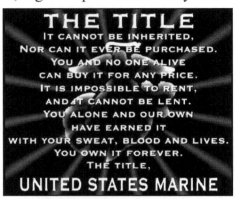

RIGHT: Bob's decorations and awards from the U.S. Marine Corps: The medals are Air Medal, Good Conduct Medal, National Defense Medal, Vietnam Campaign Medal with three stars, Vietnam Service Medal, and Combat Aircrew Wings with three stars. The ribbons are U.S. Marine Corps Combat Action, Navy Unit Commendation with three stars, Presidential Unit Citation with one star, and the Vietnam Gallantry Cross with palm.

CHAPTER TWENTY-THREE

Semper Fidelis

The Marines have landed and the situation is well in hand.

— Attributed to Richard Harding Davis (1864-1916), American author, playwright, and war correspondent

S emper Fidelis is Latin and means "Always Faithful." It's the Marine motto, as sacred to me as honor, courage, and commitment. I'm proud that I have been faithful to the core values of the Marine Corps and that those values have enhanced my spiritual path. I have pursued and found truth in paradox. I have been faithful to my spiritual name Sujay and to Gururaj's admonition to "seek balance."

Would I change anything about my life's journey? Not one thing. For all the screw-ups, the joys, and the sorrows, I wouldn't change one thing. If I did, I wouldn't be who I am now, and by and large I'm comfortable with him.

My Family

Vidya and I live in a house on a mountain in Boiling Springs, Pennsylvania, with our two Shelties, Winston and Shasta. Vidya has worked to keep the American Meditation Society going since Gururaj's death. She cherishes that responsibility and lends support to AMS courses all over the country. You may read more about AMS in Appendix A.

My sweet mother spends half the year with us in Pennsylvania and the rest of the year in Charleston, South Carolina, with my sister, Jody. My sister spent her career in advertising and marketing. She has three children who are highly educated and brilliant—a son who is a chemical engineer, a daughter who is a lawyer in D.C., and a daughter who has a master's in communications and international business and owns her own business near Charleston.

My brother, Donald Anderson, is a little younger than I am and lives in Washington State. A very smart guy and a good man. He has his own hardware business, which is doing very well. I love him very much—although I do not see him as often as I would like and I miss him.

My brother Lee Swanson continues to expand Swanson Health Products and many other businesses. Lee has earned my respect and trust through many of life's trials over the years.

As for Colleen and Crystal, our two beautiful girls, they are grown with their own beautiful children and have made wonderful lives. As all fathers do, I made a lot of mistakes rearing my two girls—nobody gives you the operating manual. But I was very dedicated to giving them the best I could and working hard to earn money to support them. That was the name of the game for me. They have always been a great joy to me and I am very proud of them both. When they were young, five or six or seven years old, they would come up to me and say, "Horsey ride, Daddy." Like any father, I'd get down on all fours and they would jump on me. And I'd buck. That's a good picture of our relationship.

Of course, I witnessed them at the age of twelve or thirteen become maniacal demons from the ninth level of hell. I didn't know what to do. Those years were traumatic for them as well as for their mother and me. That's when we were moving around a lot because I was changing jobs often. And, of course, during their teen years there was peer pressure. They did nothing really bad, just rambunctious, like crawling out of their bedroom windows to go hang out with their buddies—I did the same thing at that age. Thankfully, though, they never did anything really stupid.

Colleen finished a Bachelor of Science in Nursing at Elmira College. Something we share in common is creating processes and implementing them efficiently. When the stakes are high and there is a lot of pressure, Colleen operates really well in practical application. That's where we both excel. She is a nurse manager at UCLA Hospital. I am very proud of her.

When Crystal got to high school, she was a sad girl, highly sensitive and creative. She did not do well in ninth grade, but then something happened. She was an honors student through the rest of high school and was accepted at an honors program at St. Mary's College in Maryland. She completed the master's degree program in experimental psychology/animal behavior at the University of Tennessee.

I remember that Crystal took a summer course in calculus and aced it. She could sit at a table working for five or six hours at a time. Like her mother, she could study well and did an outstanding job on her thesis.

Really smart people, both daughters.

Colleen and Vidya are Democrats. Crystal is an Independent. I'm a conservative's conservative Republican. As you can imagine, we don't talk much at all about politics in our family.

The girls may have had some rocky times with early boyfriends, but in marriage, where it really counts, they've both struck gold. Colleen's husband, John, works in aerospace engineering; he's literally a rocket scientist. They have a little boy named Connor, four, and live in Los Angeles, California. Crystal is a wonderful mother, married to Ben, who is a corporate pilot for a Fortune 100 company. They are rearing my other two grandchildren Tyler, three, and Madelynn, two. They live in Bettendorf, Iowa.

249

BOB'S FAMILY ALBUM

Photos of Bob's beautiful daughters, Crystal and Colleen, at different ages.

250

**Bob and his beautiful wife, Vidya,
with Winston (left) and Shasta (right), their Shelties.**

TOP: Bob with daughter Colleen at her wedding. BOTTOM: Two of Bob's favorite pictures of Colleen.

ABOVE: Colleen and husband, John, and their son, Connor, in Hawaii.

BELOW: Colleen and John on their seventh wedding anniversary.

ABOVE: Crystal and her husband, Ben.

BELOW: Vidya and Bob at Crystal's and Ben's wedding.

Wedding portrait: Crystal and Ben.

ABOVE: Tyler, Crystal, Ben, and Madelynn.

BELOW: Vidya (middle) with daughters, Crystal (left) and Colleen (right).

Bob's Mom, Irene.

ABOVE: Bob with his sister, Jo, and brother, Donald Anderson.

BELOW: Bob's mother with Jo and Jo's daughter, Laura Kate.

TOP: Bob front and center surrounded by family.
BOTTOM LEFT: Brother Lee Swanson.
BOTTOM RIGHT: Bob with friend Steve Langer in Las Vegas.

259

Time with Friends

Obviously, I stay in close touch with my fellow Marines. I wear my dress uniform on special occasions, the latest when I went to Washington, D.C., to celebrate Memorial Day on May 27, 2013, in a national parade honoring military veterans, both alive and dead.

I have friends at the local firing range forty-five minutes from my home. Every weekend I shoot about 300 rounds. I'm still a great shot with both pistol and rifle (any caliber). I shoot with law enforcement, military, FBI personnel, and regular civilians. As a hobby, I also collect civilian and military weapons. Being an engineer, I love building and shooting them. They are truly mechanical marvels of precise engineering.

I change off guns each time I go to the range so I don't get any bad habits. I enjoy target practice with all of the guns in my continuously growing collection, a paradox for a man of peace.

My fascination with ordnance might just be a guy thing. I'm still sifting through the mysteries of life and still turning over new ground all the time. My Marine buddy Alan Barbour says I am what ancient Greeks called a "hoplologist." I looked up the definition, and a hoplologist studies war and weaponry from technological, functional, and behavioral viewpoints. Guess I do.

Superior marksmanship is, in fact, a form of meditation—like Zen archery. When you are on the line, you get into your preferred stance (I use a modified Weaver), bring the pistol to bear on the target, and then things get very different. Instantly there is a mental shift to no thought, no emotion.

TOP: SAIGA 12 semiautomatic shotgun.
MIDDLE: Colt M4 Carbine .223 with Holo Sight and Silencer.
BOTTOM: Springfield M1a (M-14) with Counter Sniper Scope 10x24x50.

The mind is clear throughout the process of sight alignment, breath control, and trigger squeeze. It is just a different mantra for meditating. Almost in no time, you enter "The Zone," where there is complete silence and you, the pistol, and the target become one. The weapon goes off and you do not even notice the recoil—bull's eye virtually every time.

The shooting position may change from rifle to pistol, but the zone never changes. When you are in the zone, it is impossible to miss. Now, I don't mean to say that I achieve the zone every shot—only about 90 percent of the time—but I do have targets pasted around my garage and all the centers are shot out.

Shooting is a simple and logical extension of my meditation techniques. It is effortless focus of energy, awareness, and power— letting go of outcome, staying in the zone.

I have the Marine Corps to thank for what is sacred in my life: my character. And also, for what probably isn't quite as sacred but is a helluva lot of fun: hitting the bull's eye—almost every time.

Beyond Brothers

I continue to work for Computer Aid and consider Tony Salvaggio and Mike Kucek, CAI vice president of Region 2, two of my best friends, as I've said, though we don't socialize outside work.

Lee Swanson introduced me to another person who has become a very close friend, Dr. Stephen E. Langer, a unique man who is one of the top thyroid disease physicians in the world. Steve has written a book, *Solved: The Riddle of Illness*, and is a known expert in wellness and natural healing. We share the same spiritual leanings. He comes from a background in Zen Buddhism. From my point of view, he simply uses different words for spiritual concepts I am familiar with. Our discussions can get weird and esoteric, but we have enormous fun sharing books and discussions.

When you talk about spiritual matters with many folks, for the most part nothing happens, like waving a stick in the air. But it becomes a joy to share something with friends that you love who have the same interests as you.

Like the Three Musketeers, Lee, Steve, and I bounce around together as often as our work schedules allow. Along with several other friends, we enjoy gathering informally over wine, coffee, or bottled water to exchange ideas and discuss topics of mutual intellectual interest and curiosity. We call ourselves the "Fellowship of the Mind." Rounding out the fellowship are Dr. Jovan Brkic, emeritus professor of philosophy at North Dakota State University; John Strandess, who is in marketing at Swanson's; and Bill Hansen, an attorney from Fargo, North Dakota.

We have met in restaurants, clubhouses, homes, or just about anywhere we could sit to explore realms of human knowledge and philosophy. We have all benefited greatly from these discussions.

I believe that as individuals we have gained meaningful insights from our collective knowledge and wisdom.

Punch Line

I began writing this book under a full moon at Jupiter Beach, Florida, where Vidya and I and our dogs had retreated for a couple of months in early 2010. It was the first real vacation I had attempted in years. Even so, work was always beckoning and I responded to its conference calls daily. In between, I recorded my story. Two years later, I am finishing this book at Jupiter Beach and I ask the question: Has there been any order, any direction, any reason, any purpose for the incredible diversity and intensity of all my life experiences and the resultant close and long-held relationships I've enjoyed?

Clearly, I wasn't looking for a *thing*. Because every *thing* that I found, every place I went, wasn't it.

I'd go to this country. No, that's not it.

I'd go to the bottom of the ocean. No, that's not it.

I'd go to the top of a mountain. No, that's not it.

If not all these things I've experienced, if not this tremendous symphony of ideas and sensations, then what?

Poet T.S. Eliot says it well:

> "We shall not cease from exploration
> And the end of all our exploring
> Will be to arrive where we started
> And know the place for the first time."

By the grace of God, in my long journey toward home, I've met teachers like Gururaj who helped me understand that I was running in circles across the planet looking for meaning, and that all the time what I was looking for was closer to me than my own skin.

The true meaning of life resides within each one of us. You can't read about it. No one can tell you what it is. You must experience it firsthand for yourself; then it is yours forever.

As I've tried to describe, some of the most endearing moments with Gururaj were when he screwed up the punch lines of the jokes he tried to tell, and we all laughed together with him. His laughter was music, and to be in his presence was priceless. His light-heartedness lifted us out of our heads and into the infinite love that is in us and connects us.

If my life's story has a punch line, I want it to be that I offer myself and all I have experienced to Infinite Love, which is God, and that to the best of my ability I shine a light on the path for others that they may not stumble on their journey home.

RECOMMENDED READING

Books

I Am That, talks with Sri Nisargadatta Maharaj

Beyond Freedom, talks with Sri Nisargadatta Maharaj
    Edited by Maria Jory

Prior to Consciousness, talks with Sri Nisargadatta Maharaj
    Edited by Jean Dunn

Power of Now, a guide to spiritual enlightenment
    By Eckhart Tolle

The Science of Being and the Art of Living
    by Mahararishi Mahash Yogi

The Bhagavad Gita
    Translated by Nikhilananda

Sermon on the Mount according to Vedanta

The Gospel According to Ramakrishna
    Translated by Swami Nikhilananda

The Hero with a Thousand Faces
    by Joseph Campbell

The Tao of Physics
    by Fritjof Capra

Practicing Peace in Times of War
    by Pema Chödrön

Theory of Relativity
    by Albert Einstein

Brief History of Time
    by Stephen Hawking

Starship Troopers
    by Robert Heinlein

Physics of Motion
> by Sir Isaac Newton

Universe, The Definitive Visual Guide
> General Editor Martin Rees

The Art of War
> by Sun Tzu

Books by Gururaj Ananda Yogi

From Darkness to Light

God and Man

The Master Reflects

Web Sites

Space.com website:
> http://www.space.com/52-the-expanding-universe-from-the-big-bang-to-today.html

Atlas of the Universe website:
> http://www.atlasoftheuniverse.com/

Bob's Blog:
> www.itservicemanagement-itil.com/

Computer Aid Inc. website:
> http://www.compaid.com/

U.S. Marine Corps website:
> http://www.marines.com/history-heritage

VMO-2 website:
> http://www.angelfire.com/va/cherrydeuce/

NASA website:
> http://map.gsfc.nasa.gov/universe/index.html

American Meditation Society website:
> www.AmericanMeditationSociety.org

APPENDIX A

The American Meditation Society Today

AMS has a beautiful website (americanmeditationsociety.org) and is publishing audio recordings, video recordings, and books to perpetuate the teachings of Gururaj Ananda Yogi. Gururaj wanted people to know that it is our destiny to find our own inner guru, or the direct connection to the heart, the superconscious level of the mind.

AMS states its goals: "AMS set out to carry on the teachings of this great spiritual master in the way he requested. He taught that, to be truly effective, meditation and spiritual practices must be individually prescribed and then taught by a qualified instructor. We still uphold those standards. We conduct retreats in which we meditate together and study the vast body of recorded wisdom he left as part of his legacy. We have local meditation meetings where we cook, eat, and laugh together. We support one another when life puts us through our own difficult practices. In short, we do our best to embody the principles he taught us, to live accordingly, and share these teachings with others."

One thing that distinguishes Gururaj's message is that he derived personalized techniques for each individual from deep insight into the core of the new meditator.

Now, many may be quite skeptical at using such words, but for me if it works, I don't care if Daffy Duck whispered into his ear. Over the last thirty-five years of doing his meditation practices, I can tell you truthfully from my own personal experience that they work. As they say, the proof is in the pudding.

When Gururaj passed, there were only, as far as I know, three people that he taught how to derive personal techniques. These people had been with him for more than twelve years, sometimes 24/7. One of them was my wife, Vidya.

He did not train me. That wasn't my job, he said.

He personally trained Rajesh(in UK), Roopa Morosani, and Vidya (in the USA) to do what he did. Maybe there is a limited timeline on perpetuating Gururaj's techniques. No one knows. However, the teachings are eternal. Truth always emerges as it needs to, when it needs to. It rises and falls and there is no way to know why it is that way. We are judging by so little information, so little understanding.

A much deeper and wider game is being played here than we can see. Energies move in a certain way and at a certain time because they must. It is not up to us to decide how they are suppose to go. Like hydrogen atoms collecting and collapsing to form a star, these subtler energies have the same deal. They move and flow and go exactly as they are supposed to. It's not up to our puny little 10 percent minds with such a limited vision and scope to judge that which we do not understand.

So many AMS folks are part of my extended family circle, because of our shared experiences with Gururaj. And so many more worldwide. You forge the deepest and longest lasting bonds with those whom you've learned you can trust over time. I love everyone of them. I'm very glad that I'm taking this life journey with them. We've laughed when things were funny and supported each other when times were hard. Were it not for Gururaj, I wouldn't have met any of them.

APPENDIX B

(As referenced in CHAPTER THIRTEEN)

GURURAJ AND I WROTE LETTERS back and forth when he was in South Africa and I was at home in the U.S. I would like to share a few letters that I think, though written to me, he wrote to everyone. They speak to all of us, not just to one of us.

From the Desk of Gururaj Ananda Yogi—8/14/81
My beloved Sujay and Vidya,
It is so unimaginable to think I am thousands of miles away from you and yet feel as if I am with you both in such close embrace. In the plane, going into meditation, I even felt Vidya stitching on a troublesome pajama button. And you saying so softly in my ears, "Bapuji let us go to bed now, you need the rest." I know you said this in your deep concern for an unwell body, but I just wanted to share a close closeness in just a few days, that may never be again in this life. I want to thank you for your kind hospitality and looking after me so well. What more to say when the unsaid word is said.

I arrived home on the 10th August—doing things in Johannesburg. Exhaustion had built up, and I collapsed for a few days and the doctor treated me. I am so well now. Fit as a fiddle and back into action. You, no doubt, beloved Sujay will say "Take Care." You can bet your arse I do...So do not worry about anything at all.

Vidya, please phone Phyllis for me. "All tight knots are slowly being untied, and it is about time that she puts her ideas of perfection down with the toilet paper." Human life is never a perfection, but a process towards that. Enjoy ! Enclosed is a poem for you all. I love you. Bapuji. Please look after my mother Irene - I love her. And the children remain with me at all times.

From the Desk of Gururaj Ananda Yogi—12/31/83
My Beloved Sujay,
I LOVE YOU

From the Desk of Gururaj Ananda Yogi—5/20/84
Beloved Sujay,
Thanks for your lovely letter received today. You are well aware of our deep love and bond so it would only be a repetition to say, "I love you."

Biren has taken out Rajesh and Jasmini for the day. I am feeling too weak to go out. My whole body is trembling and am going back to bed now.

Sitting in the lounge, looking at your UNICORN, it gives me a great sense of stamina.

Thanks also to you beloved Vids for your letters. We do not need psycho junk which will not help anyone. My mission in life as is yours is to impart spirituality. Thousands of people around the globe have benefited by knowing love, and knowing this is knowing God.

The main idea now in my last days of life is to spread my words in printed form. This could mean that a god lived amongst us and every word he spoke stays immortal.

I love you both, my beloved selves.

Love, Bapuji

From the Desk of Gururaj Ananda Yogi
July 23, 1984, 11 p.m.
My beloved, beloved Sujay,
Thank you for your tape. I have listened to it over and over again.
Your poem has really touched the depth of my heart. YOU ARE A
GENIUS!

I LOVE YOU MY BELOVED SON - ABHIMANYU.

I wrote to you a few days ago which I am sure you must have received.

My deepest love to Vidya, Mom, Coll and Crys.

All are keeping well here including me. Take things easy; do not over-
work yourself. This world will still be functioning even when you and
I are not around.

A great big hug to the goddess Vidya DEVI on my behalf and the kids.

I love you all a million times more than what you may realize.

Bapuji

ॐ

From the Desk of Gururaj Ananda Yogi—9/14/84
Beloved Sujay,
It was nice to hear your voice on the phone the other day. You sounded
so cheerful; yet I could detect some measure of "agony and ecstasy"
through your voice. I was very pleased about this, for have I not
traveled the same road through many lifetimes?

The undulating waves in its turmoil will always be there. The secret I
have found is to participate in the turmoil but yet be still. The rock
stands still only the waves move.

Yet paradoxically the rock also moves in its own stillness—unaware of its own awareness. When the awareness comes that I am not This, but I am That; and that, "THAT IS THIS." Analysis comes from the mind, mergence comes from the heart. The heart to heart, the heart in heart, until even the heart disappears—no passion, no emotion, no attachment, no comprehension of what these qualities are all about—just existing in the impulse of existence which is the energy called God.

Now, to come to the practical side of things. I am busy on a theory with a temporary title: ENERGY LEVELS IN RELATION TO PERPETUAL MOTION—A NON-PHYSICS VIEWPOINT. This is going to knock the rubbish out of many old thoughts up to now.

I love you my beloved Sujay. When I see you in November, I would like to work out a plan where we could promise to write each other once a week (with immediate replies) on intellectual subjects.

I say old chap, you have a great brain (don't feel flattered).

See you soon, love to Mom, Vidya, Coll & Crys and the same amount to you in full measure.

That barman at McGees must not short-tot you. I would never do that.

All my love,
Your Bapuji

From the Desk of Gururaj Ananda Yogi—10/10/84
My darling son, beloved Sujay,
I have not heard from you and no letters from Vidya either. I am sure it must be because of your trip to New York.

Now, on a more philosophical note, the Vedantic proposition of Maya is Maya itself. How can an unreal mind recognize unreality? If anything is unreal then the omnipresence of Divinity falls away. Non-reality presupposes the non-existence of the underlying subtle factor which is incomprehensible to the senses.

The only solution is to be in contact at all times with the subtle factor and this connection brings about in its wake an infusion of the subtle with the gross and, so, spontaneously, makes everything alive. Unreality is destroyed, only reality exists but with a quality of love and bliss. This is the fourth dimension. If this is neglected life is incomplete. The incompleteness is but another name for misery and turmoil.

All is real—for reality is perfection; if we just move one step away from temporary sense-gratification, which even at its best, cannot help.

Life is immortal. It is never destroyed. But people in chameleon form change colors, but the chameleon remains alive.

Love you my son and love to Mom, Vids & Kids.

Bapuji

P.S. NICE TITLE FOR A BOOK: "THE SUBTLE FACTOR"

From the Desk of Gururaj Ananda Yogi—10/26/84
My beloved Sujay,
Just received your letter of the 3rd. I too, as you, become speechless, though mind in myriad thoughts abound; the river flows on and on through crags & rocks to find that which is still unfound.

We reach the ocean to find life's river's end. Do we not go through every bend? Our doing's to mend!

The river's life is filled with frailty and folly—rushing and gushing—shall it meet up with the stormy waves of that ocean, or subside in the silence within?

Hand in hand we go, yet neither coming or going, just to be here and knowing I LOVE YOU.

Bapuji

LOVE TO MOM VIDS & KIDS

From the Desk of Gururaj Ananda Yogi—1/5/85—3 a.m.
My dearest beloveds—Suj, Vids & Kids,
It was so wonderful to speak to you both the other day. It filled my heart with such great joy. The last letter from Suj was so beautiful. I read it over and over again. The clarity of thought, construction and wisdom was superb. Suj, you must really start writing a book on any subject. Does not matter what—but just start in your spare time. I will be writing to you soon. Vidya, you must keep a copy of our letters.

Harish, Anjoli, Deepo & Grace came home to tea last week & Satish & Mariana came home for dinner. They are leaving back to Australia next week. Everyone is coming back to Bapuji with so so much love. As a matter of fact Harish wants to start up a center for us in Cape Town—we shall see!

Enclosed is but a sampling of the cards received. (There is a whole box full, but postage would be exorbitant if I should send them all.) This is to show you that our work is not in vain. Our efforts are worthwhile, as it should be.

The holiday season had been hectic. I hardly reached home from my trip and I had visitors from USA & other places to look after. No time to rest. On the other social activity side I distributed at Xmas 100 food parcels to the very poor. The family & I sat up nights to make up the food boxes. You saw some of the areas. I also gave R500.00 to the Youth Society for sporting equipment. Though I have financial problems, I always give a percentage of what I earn for some good work. Real joy in life comes from giving even if we have to struggle. To serve man in total honesty and purity is to serve God.

Well my darlings, the page has run out. You are going to have a super, super 1985.

I LOVE YOU,

Bapuji

∽

From the Desk of Gururaj Ananda Yogi—no date
My beloved Suj,

SOME OBSERVATIONS:

You have a very keen, perceptive mind much given to intellectual analysis, but still wanting to reach that which is un-analyzable. Carry on beloved, for I see you have strong desire for the mergence of the relative with the absolute. You know so well that they coexist, and you try and see it all with an inner eye and sometimes become confused...that should I be down here or really up there.

Much love,
Your Bapuji

From the Desk of Gururaj Ananda Yogi—no date

My beloved Sujay,
Beloved one

You shall be the one that would carry my message to the world. I want nothing at all from you but just your love and devotion. There are millions you can earn which you can use for any purpose you like, but you are the only one that will carry forward the wisdom imparted from me, which contains such great love, which totally contains me. I love you, my darling my Vivekananda. Be worthy of your name, Sujay, And you will find total peace within yourself.

Always always always.

For you and I ARE Me.

I love you, My beloved Sujay.

(back side of letter)

Though he has served a purpose

Robert is but a shell.

When the Great One breaks through

to wing full-formed from those bonds

he will not give a backward glance

278

(As referenced in CHAPTER SIXTEEN)

Text of *Computerworld* Article

'25 Time-Test Truths About IT Support
Read 'Em and Reap Better Productivity, Service, and
Overall Performance'

I've worked for Computer Aid for about a quarter century. I'm especially proud of my contribution to CAI's intellectual Properties. In large part, because of the industry's interest in our company's products, I was published in the December 2008 and the February 2007 issues of *Computerworld* and generated favorable responses from the magazine's readers worldwide. The following article I wrote for the 2007 issue nicely summarizes the integrated approach I take to my work and my clients. It is wholly influenced by my spiritual practice.

Webster's Dictionary defines an axiom as "a self-evident truth that requires no proof." Over the course of decades in IT, I've discovered 25 axioms about the IT support environment. Being aware of these can help you design support processes that will make sense, work well, and improve your team's performance. Here are some of the great truths I've learned and how your team can apply them for better IT support.

1. The estimate a user hears is the estimate the user will remember; the date a user hears is the date the user will remember. Never give a verbal estimate or date you're not willing to live and die by.

2. Work without defined boundaries is work that may never end. Don't say, "I'm working on it," without qualifying when it will be done and, if necessary, why it won't be done on time.

3. The support team is most vulnerable when moving something into production. Just the right amount of constructive paranoia is a

good thing. Are you sure the right modules and versions moved into production? Check again!

4. Users have selective amnesia. Always get sign-off or written approval.

5. Nothing will be done and nothing will work unless you invest some personal time to check it. Assume that, and you will never be surprised.

6. "No!" isn't a constructive response. Never use it when a request for work or assistance is made. Instead, say, "Let me review it, and I'll get back to you by Tuesday." Then think about it; you just might be able to help.

7. What you can't measure, you can't control. Define service-level goals, and capture measurement data at its source. Compare the "should" to the "is."

8. You can't come up with an accurate estimate without knowing the number and complexity of the functions required. Deconstruct functional requirements, even for small requests.

9. The fox is not a good henhouse guard. Don't quality-control your own work. Always have independent verification.

10. The test environment is not the production environment. Never assume that because it works in the former, it will work in the latter.

11. If you buy it, you own it. If you take the support call, it's your responsibility to make sure it's completed successfully.

12. Critique is positive; blame is negative. Don't blame; figure out how the group can do it better.

13. Murphy's Law is optimistic. Even the most carefully planned and executed activities will go astray at the worst possible moment. Always be vigilant, flexible, and prepared.

14. Effective communication will smooth over a lot of problems or prevent potential problems from happening. Communicate potential problems or newly discovered issues to your colleagues and management team right away. Be proactive, not reactive.

15. Nobody likes surprises. Communication changes to all who will be affected.

16. Your memory isn't trustworthy; neither is the user's. Don't trust memory; write it down.

17. Work isn't completed until you get verification from the user that it's completed. Never assume.

18. If you don't clearly define expectations, you will get what you deserve, not what you need. Be specific about what you want and when you want it, what you will deliver and when you will deliver it.

19. Users are customers, not problems. Treat them that way.

20. Perception is reality. Always get feedback on what you think you communicated. Never assume that your perception is their reality.

21. Accountability without authority leads to failure. If someone is being held accountable, give him the authority he needs to succeed.

22. It's easy to see problems; solutions are tougher. Never go to someone with a problem in one hand unless you have at least one solution in the other hand.

23. Your common sense is not always someone else's common sense. Don't assume that just because it's obvious to you, it will be obvious to others.

24. Technology doesn't always work as it's supposed to. Develop test strategies that thoroughly exercise the required operational limits of any technology on which the business depends.

25. Irretrievable data corruption usually occurs on files that are not backed up. Always back up your systems and data on a regular schedule.

If you design your IT support processes with these truths in mind and get your group to live by them, you'll improve your productivity, the quality of service delivered, and overall performance.

APPENDIX D
(As referenced in CHAPTER NINETEEN)

Additional Intuitive Writings
by Sujay Anderson

Silence Is . . .

The sound of a snowflake falling on a cold winter day,

The peace that passeth understanding,

The stillness wherein all conflicts are resolved,

The mystery which confounds the mind but is experienced by the heart,

The canvas upon which dreams are painted,

The beginning, the journey and the destination,

All of these and none of these, Silence Is . . .

A Dream

A dream is life turned inward

Life is a dream turned outward . . .

Love Alone Abides

Time, fickle as a butterfly's flight eludes my grasp.

My form, as mist in dawns early light fades and is seen no more.

My love alone abides.

Love's gentle light shining eternally to illumine the face of God.

It is in this sweet vision I find thee beloved . . .

The Invisible Sword

Harkin, oh warriors of Truth. Listen as I tell you of the sword which is sharper than the finest edge, suppler than a willow branch, mightier than the greatest of weapons forged by the masters.

It will never break, loose its keen edge or fail you in moments of need.

It is that sword which cuts through the bonds of ignorance opens the closed heart and cleaves the veil of illusion.

It is the invisible sword of discrimination.

It is the weapon of your birthright, forged within you at the time of your making.

Oh warriors, listen well, to be the master of this sword, you must practice constantly and with mindfulness.

Of what good is the greatest of swords if it is kept in its sheath?

Battle tirelessly and with courage. Every thought, every feeling, every breath, every movement must be tested against the edge of the sword of discrimination.

All that is True to your essential nature will not be pierced or cut, but will become one with the blade.

With time and diligent practice, all that is false and illusion will be cut asunder until only your true Self remains.

The invisible sword of discrimination merges within the bright splendor of this true Self.

The final battle won—what is there left to cut?
You have merged with the Truth of all that is or ever will be.

The sword has served its purpose, it is now sheathed glory.

Oh, warriors, you may rest for a time...Until called again.

Printed in Great Britain
by Amazon

57618843R00169